LoveEd
PARENT GUIDE

RAISING KIDS THAT ARE STRONG, SMART AND PURE

LoveEd
PARENT GUIDE

RAISING KIDS THAT ARE STRONG, SMART AND PURE

Nihil Obstat
Reverend John Balluff, STD
Censor Deputatus
April 29, 2016

Permission to Publish
Most Reverend Joseph Siegel, DD, STL
Vicar General
Diocese of Joliet
May 2, 2016

ISBN: 978-1-5051-0930-6

Published in the United States by
Saint Benedict Press
PO Box 410487
Charlotte, NC 28241
www.SaintBenedictPress.com

Printed in the United States of America

Contents

A Note to Parents

Dear Parents,

Parenting is not easy today. Both you and your children are bombarded with constant pressures. It's no secret that our culture has an obsession with sex but doesn't really understand how to live a true and faithful love. Movies, television, the Internet, and music expose children at an early age to a twisted perception of God's plan for romance and sexual relationships. It can be difficult to remember that God has a good plan for love-giving and life-giving.

Family life is more complicated than ever in this age of information, materialism, utilitarianism, constant pressures, traveling sports, and busy-ness. Our culture is experiencing record low marriage rates and record high divorce rates. Yet we know that there is a truth behind family life that we strive to live—both for ourselves and the common good.

This cultural situation challenges us daily and affects our ongoing decisions.

Are you concerned when:
- You can't find a modest outfit for your ten-year-old daughter?
- Your eight-year-old has a few friends over, and they disappear into the bedroom with their tablet or computers?
- Your eleven-year-old asks to hang out at the shopping center with his friends, both girls and boys, unsupervised?
- Your thirteen-year-old is allowed to view an R-rated movie at a friend's house?
- Your inquisitive seven-year-old brings up sexual questions after seeing a TV commercial or hearing something at school?

Parents, you are not alone!

So, what is a parent to do? Do we go with the flow and accept this as the real world today? Do we trust our parental instincts when we feel uncomfortable with a situation? Do we look to our Faith while making important parenting decisions?

Years ago, we baptized our children into the Body of Christ—the Church—and promised to parent them in the light of Christ. Our children need our love and help to stand strong in their faith in order to experience the fullness of life that comes only through Jesus Christ.

Your child looks to you for guidance. Studies show that children and teens desire more time with their families. They want love, limits, and discipline even if they appear to resist. It takes effort and scheduling for parents to make faith and family relationships a priority, but when you make that effort, your whole family benefits.

LoveEd is designed to help you have deeper, more meaningful conversations that can forge an important relationship between you and your children surrounding the topics of love, life, sexuality, and purity. *LoveEd* helps you empower your children with the truth as they enter the various stages of development so that they can become the people God wants them to be and learn to love according to His plan.

You can do this! And *LoveEd* is here to help.

Sincerely,
Coleen Kelly Mast, MS
Author, wife, mother of five, and host of EWTN Radio's Mast Appeal

Why LoveEd? Why Now?

Nothing Can Replace the Family

The family is the first school of living, and the influence received inside the family is decisive for the future development of the individual.

—Pope St. John Paul II, Message for World Day of Peace, 1998

The Strength of Love

In family life, we need to cultivate that strength of love which can help us fight every evil threatening it. The Christian ideal, especially in families, is a love that never gives up.

—Pope Francis, *Amoris Laetitia*, 2016

Love Can Transform

The vocation to love is a wonderful thing, it is the only force that can truly transform the cosmos, the world.

—Pope Benedict XVI, World Meeting of Families in Milan, 2012

A Union of Persons in the Image of God

The word of God tells us that the family is entrusted to a man, a woman and their children, so that they may become a communion of persons in the image of the union of the Father, the Son and the Holy Spirit.

—Pope Francis, *Amoris Laetitia*, 2016

Sexuality Information Always Belongs in the Context of Love

Information regarding sexuality is provided in the broadest context of education for love.

—The National Directory for Catechesis, United States Bishops

An Introduction to LoveEd

This Parent Guide is part of *LoveEd*, a multimedia program that helps children discover the amazing truth about human sexuality. It combines the beautiful teachings of the Catholic Church with scientific truth to teach children what they need to know at appropriate age levels. The goal of *LoveEd* is to help parents raise kids who are *strong*, *smart*, and *pure*.

In this book and the parent videos, we've included information to help you teach these topics at home while your children are young. Together, the book and videos will help guide your children to a Christian understanding of virtuous love and human sexuality.

Parent Training

The Parent Training Event has seven video segments completed in four parts. Small group discussion time is planned between these segments, guided by questions in this book. The videos include parent testimonials, as well as the author relaying God's plan for love with practical applications for today.

- The seven videos for parents cover:
- An Introduction to *LoveEd*
- The Cultural Context
- Church Teaching on Human Sexuality
- The First Stage of Love Learning: Early Childhood
- The Second Stage of Love Learning: Years of Innocence
- The Third Stage of Love Learning: Prepubescence
- The Fourth Stage of Love Learning: Adolescence

Parent/Child Events

Following the Parent Training, *LoveEd* consists of four age- and gender-based Parent/Child Events with accompanying student guides to help facilitate discussion with your child. Like this Parent Program, each Parent/Child Event follows a template of watching video segments and turning to the guides for further reading and discussion.

The four *LoveEd* Parent/Child Events are:
- Boys Level 1 - Father and Son at Puberty (Ages 9-11)
- Boys Level 2 - Father and Son at Young Adolescence (Ages 11-14)
- Girls Level 1 - Mother and Daughter at Puberty (Ages 9-11)
- Girls Level 2 - Mother and Daughter at Young Adolescence (Ages 11-14)

If the parent of the same gender is not available, a close and loving substitute can assist, or the opposite-sex parent can foster these conversations if necessary.

Each Parent/Child Event is divided into six segments called "Acts," though the last one does not have a video component and is simply a prayer and blessing ceremony. Each level and gender's video has appropriate differences, but in all four groups, the five acts have these general themes:

- **Act 1** meets your child at their level with a short film about the struggles of growing up from a kid's perspective.
- **Act 2** introduces the way that love is learned in the context of family, friendship, and romance, with the virtues that are to be learned in each circle of love.
- **Act 3** zooms out beyond earth to tell the story of God's divine love. It shows how God's love redeemed us.
- **Act 4** includes age and gender appropriate biological information parents need to discuss with their preteens or teens. Both age groups review the puberty information, how to manage it, and how our changing bodies are part of God's amazing plan. The adolescent Level 2 teaches about God's plan for marriage, the marriage act, conception, and fetal development, clearly teaching how our changing bodies are part of God's amazing plan.
- **Act 5** gives parents and their children the opportunity to discuss the practical and moral advice they need for their journey forward. There will be obstacles ahead that need management with the help they will get from their family, friends, and the Church to guide them on their way.
- **Act 6** prepares for the important follow-up sessions at home and includes a closing prayer and parent blessing of the child.

In general, these segments cover, among other things, the following topics:
- The scientific realities of puberty.
- Daily struggles in social and family life.
- The "Circles of Love" and where children fit into their family, friendships, and future circle of romantic love.
- How children can prepare *now* to become pure and chaste.
- Where children fit into God's plan for the world.
- How children can strive to develop their talents to give their lives back to God, whether through celibacy or marriage.
- Age-appropriate details about the reproductive system.
- For younger teens, scientific information that explains how God created us male and female in order to serve Him.

After each video, you can discuss privately and with sensitivity what they already know and what they need to understand, both scientifically and morally.

Throughout this entire process, marriage and the marriage act are presented as sacred, with uplifting language. Likewise, conception and fetal development are explained to help understand the dignity of the human person from the moment of conception. The goal is to convey the awe of God's creation and our responsibility to use our sexual powers for real love.

LoveEd is designed to empower you, the parent, to be the primary educator of your child with the assistance and wisdom of the Catholic Church. The Church, founded by Jesus Christ, is here to enlighten us with God's truths, help us understand them, support us in living them, and offer us God's mercy as we struggle. It is in our daily struggles to live a life of virtue that we see its importance for our own children. You, as a parent, are the one who is in the best position to show your child that the love of God and a life of virtue are the foundations of human happiness.

At-Home Follow-Up

This part of the program is very important because there is so much more for your son or daughter to process and discuss than could be accomplished at the Parent/Child Event. There will likely be some topics he or she will feel more comfortable discussing later, after they have time to process what they learned. Your continued open communication will benefit both of you to create the best relationship possible, especially when they run into difficult decisions or trials. Even though you are busy, prioritize this special time spent with your soon-to-be young man or woman.

How and Where Do We Use This Program?

Parents are irreplaceable as teachers of the specific details of physiology and intimate morality.[1] The Church has always supported this concept. The Church can also assist parents directly and can assist their children with catechetical formation in faith and morals.[2] This program meets that need in a positive and concrete way by providing the intimate details in sacred language. It will help parents select the right words that respect a child's innocence, and yet still give the information they need to understand that morality and science are both interconnected and are a part of God's plan.

LoveEd should always involve you, the parent, working alongside your child. But it has been designed for all educational settings:

1. At the school or parish with group viewing and private conversation between parent and child*
2. At parent/child retreats*
3. At home within the family

*A Facilitator Guide will assist with the group process.

Turning Sex Ed into LoveEd—More Than Just "The Talk"

LoveEd teaches, "love is sacrificing yourself for the good of another." Parents know that real love requires sacrifice. We learn about this sacrificial love in many ways:

- First, from God who loves us and created us.
- Second, from our families who care for us.
- Third, from our extended family, relatives, and friends.
- Fourth, as we mature to adulthood, our romantic desires may lead us to married love.

The focus of learning in the *LoveEd* program concentrates on the virtues, knowing that many virtues are required along the way to adulthood before a person is capable of making a lifetime commitment of love.

Students learn that they are to develop their talents as a gift of love back to God and share their talents with the people they meet in order to reflect God's love to everyone. They learn that they are to become a gift of love.

One of the six segments of *LoveEd* for each age and gender teaches about the science of life. The material is sensitively and prudently presented and expresses the awe and wonder of our Creator. These teachings help everyone keep in perspective that physical changes are part of one's normal personal growth and physical love is part of a whole personal relationship of married love between a man and a woman.

The cultural confusion today regarding sexuality often narrowly associates the word "love" merely with sexual activity or lust. *LoveEd* is designed to help our children understand a broader concept of what God's love is all about: that it is given back to Him, learned through the family, experienced in romantic relationships, and expressed through marriage. God calls all people, whether single or married, to learn to love one another and share His love in appropriate ways.

In order for love to be pure and real, we have to practice the virtues, particularly the virtue of chastity. The United States Bishops Conference, in their document on chastity formation, teaches us that "education for chastity is more than a call to abstinence. It requires:

- Understanding the need for a family environment of love, virtue, and respect for the gifts of God.
- Learning the practice of decency, modesty, and self-control.
- Guiding sexual instincts toward loving service of others.
- Recognizing one's embodied existence as male or female as a gift from God.
- Discerning one's vocation to marriage, or to chaste life, to celibate priesthood, or to consecrated virginity for the sake of the Kingdom of Heaven."[3]

Was Sexuality Really God's Idea?

Of course sexuality was God's idea! After all, He created the sexes—male and female—to be complementary.

Sexuality is part of God's plan for our happiness. He created us male and female so that each new person could be born into a family, born of the love of a man and woman committed to one another for life in the sacrament of marriage. He gave men and women the desire for one another and asks them to fulfill these desires within the sacrament. God gives each couple the graces of the Sacrament of Matrimony to live out their married life with virtue. Since sin entered the world, however, God's perfect plan for marriage doesn't always happen as it should. This causes a great deal of pain for the whole family. These disappointments do not mean that sexuality in marriage is not a good idea; it means that it is not always easy to live up to. But God, in His great love and mercy, can still restore all things to His goodness. God always wants what's best for our family happiness, and sexuality in marriage is part of His wonderful plan.

Teach Your Child Who They Are—Affirm Their Identity as a Child of God

All the teachings of human sexuality are rooted in who we are: children of God. For these teachings to take root, your child should be grounded in this basic truth.

If your child asks, "Who am I?" the clear answer is, "I am a child of God almighty, loved by Him. What defines me is my relationship to God. Just imagine this: I have the privilege of being a child of God! God has loved me so much that He has adopted me as His child! This is awe-inspiring. This is who I really am, and I then act accordingly, as Christ taught me."

Your child's search for identity in adolescence may involve a discovery of his or her talents and how to develop those gifts so as to serve God, but this is all rooted in his or her identity as His child, deeply and personally loved by Him.

Not only are your children loved by God, but they deserve to be loved here on earth. Your children learn about loving relationships from you. As they grow, you teach them about relationships that are good for them and relationships that are bad for them. The theology and morality of sexuality is rooted in their need to love and be loved as God loves us.

These Godly Concepts Might Sound Good, But Have You Seen the Real World Out There?

People who think of sexual union as just a pleasurable activity might think that the Church is trying to impose some restrictions on their freedom. People who know and live the truth and goodness of human sexuality may wonder how there could be so much misunderstanding and misuse of this wonderful gift. Many people live somewhere between these two ideas, yet are always seeking to know and live the truth.

Your children may have an intellectual conflict between what they are seeing around them and God's plan for them. They may wonder, *If God's plan for human sexuality is so beautiful . . .*

- Why do so many people treat human sexuality as if it were something dirty or forbidden?
- Why do many treat their sexuality as if their bodies were playthings made only for pleasure?
- Why do people act sexually in ways that ignore God's grace, as though we were mere animals, not human beings made in God's image and likeness?
- Why are parents often afraid to bring up the subject?

Your good example and your ongoing conversations can help your children know and defend these answers over the years. The discussion of these topics will probably bring up questions from your child regarding relatives, acquaintances, celebrities and even ourselves who may not have always lived out their sexuality in the context of God's love. With great charity and mercy toward these people (especially toward yourself!), you can continue to clarify the truth and beauty of God's plan. Help your children form their consciences now so they will not be swayed by the bad example of others, however popular those poor examples may be (in the case of celebrities) or however much you may love those who are not good examples.

What If I Haven't Followed Catholic Teachings Myself?

If you already live the beautiful gift of married sexuality—faithful, loving, and open to life—well then, rejoice and thank God for His blessings and grace! But realistically, that is not true of most Catholic parents today because we live in a culture that has miseducated us about sexuality.

We're all sinners in one way or another. Yet some sins have more profound and longer lasting consequences than others. This is true of sexual sin, always so popular throughout the ages. The Church helps us avoid some of the negative consequences of sin by teaching us the boundaries that God has set for us in the Ten Commandments. God's commands are meant not to keep us from having fun but rather to help us live without hurting ourselves or others. And even when we sin, God is merciful and desires our happiness.

Parents often ask, "Do I need to tell my children about my sexual sins of the past?" No, you do not need to confess your sexual past to your children. Does it help to unload your baggage on them? No, not at all. Be not afraid. If you have already sought forgiveness for any past sexual sins and have experienced the freedom of God's redeeming grace, you will discover the strength and credibility to teach the truth to your children, whether or not you have lived it yourself. The Sacrament of Reconciliation forgives sins and opens the soul for healing. "If we acknowledge our sins, he is faithful and just and will forgive our sins and cleanse us from every wrongdoing" (1 Jn 1:9).

One of the outstanding examples of forgiveness for sexual sin was King David in the Old Testament. King David committed adultery with Bathsheba while her husband was out fighting for David's kingdom. When she becomes pregnant with his child, David tries to cover it up by having her husband, Uriah, killed on the front lines of battle (see 2 Sm 11). After the prophet Nathan helps him see the error of his ways, David repents of his grievous sin. With fasting and prayer, he turned to God for forgiveness. David was so moved by the mercy of God that he wrote many of the psalms we read in the Bible today.

Your situation may be either different or very similar to David's:

- Maybe you are divorced, but you still believe in the commitment of marriage and want your children to be prepared for the best and most faithful marriage they can have.

- Maybe you experienced sex before marriage, but you want to spare your own children the negative consequences of that experience, or you are now aware that there are so many more consequences to premarital sex than anyone knew back then.

- Maybe you are a single parent and find it a challenge to practice chastity while you are dating. Yet you know your children look up to you and want to be like you when they grow up.

- Maybe you used birth control or had an abortion at a time when you didn't fully understand the spiritual implications.

No one can change his or her past, but each person, with the grace of God, has the power to affect his or her future and train his or her children in the way of truth.

Many great saints have struggled with lust and won the battle over sexual temptations. They found their strength in God and their respect for His beautiful plan for sexuality, rather than in denial, excuses, or repression. St. Augustine, a brilliant theologian and a Doctor of the Church, was once immersed in sexual sin and lived with a woman who bore his child, all before his amazing conversion to Christianity. In his famous work *Confessions*, he said, "Lust indulged became a habit, and habit unresisted became a necessity." St. Francis also conquered sins of the flesh. He was known to roll in the snow to calm his passionate desires before the days of cold showers.

Other saints were martyred while standing up for God's plan for marriage. St. John the Baptist boldly told King Herod that he should not be sleeping with his brother's wife, and he was thus beheaded at the mistress's wish (see Mk 6:14–29). St. Thomas More was a lawyer in England and a councilor to King Henry VIII. The king had many marriages and refused to accept the Catholic Church's teachings. He tried to convince the leaders in Rome to grant him invalid annulments. St. Thomas More stood with the Church and was accused of treason against the king; he was ultimately put to death for defending God's plan for sacramental marriage and faithfulness.

God's Plan for Mercy: Plead Guilty and Be Forgiven

Parents, as teachers of your children, you can gain great confidence in the mercy of God. With God, when you plead guilty, you are forgiven. This is the opposite of the court system where you plead guilty and are punished. Jesus already took the punishment for our sins. If you discover that you're sorry for any inappropriate ways you have acted in the past, please know that the arms of God's mercy are waiting in the confessional through the priest, God's representative of His mercy here on earth. In the Sacrament of Penance, we can find forgiveness, healing, comfort, and peace. God gives us the grace to strengthen us each day. This strength will help us teach our children about God's plan for love.

Strong, Smart, and Pure: Rewind

Strong: Your love for your children and the grace of God will give you the strength to teach them about real love.

Smart: *LoveEd* will give you the information you need to teach your children about growing up according to God's plan for love, life, and virtue.

Pure: Pure hearts and minds are what you want for your kids, and *LoveEd* will help you give them the tools to be the best person God wants them to be.

Strong, Smart, and Pure: Fast Forward

Strong: The information you receive will give you the strength and commitment to help your family know the truths that counter the disordered messages of the culture.

Smart: The teachings of God, as found in Scripture, the Church, and our very bodies, will give you the understanding of God's beautiful intent for marriage and sexuality.

Pure: When you teach your children why and how they can remain pure, you give them the tools for a life filled with the joy of committing to God's intentions for them.

LoveEd Parent Training

Whether you are embarking on the *LoveEd* Parent Training in a group setting or going through the program at home, alone or with your spouse, now is the time to complete the Video & Discussion portion. The videos feature author Coleen Kelly Mast along with a variety of parents who share their experience and commitment to living out Catholic wisdom on love and sexuality.

There are four parts to this portion of the program. Each follows the same pattern:
1. Watch the short video (or group of videos).
2. Answer the discussion questions that follow.

If you are doing this program on your own, we invite you to reflect on the questions and write down any thoughts you have as you move through the material.

Whether you are with a group, with your spouse, or by yourself, we congratulate you on taking this most important step to educating your child in love!

PART I

Watch the *Introductory Video: Why LoveEd* (4 minutes) and discuss the following questions. Make notes where it will help you formulate plans to implement these lessons with your children later.

1. Think back to your own childhood. How did you learn about sex? What role did your parents play in your sex education? What role did the Church play, if any, either through Catholic school or religious education classes?

_____

_____

_____

2. Identify several misconceptions of love and sex that are coming into your home from the outside world. Discuss ways you can combat these misconceptions.

_____

_____

_____

3. As a parent, name at least three teachings you want your children to know about sexuality.

4. What are some steps you can take to enact a plan for helping your children learn the things you mentioned in number 3?

5. Reflect and discuss how much you know about the beauty of the Catholic Church's teachings on sexuality. Do you think you could explain or defend them to someone who thinks the teachings are just a bunch of useless rules?

PART II

Watch the next two videos, *The Cultural Context* (6 minutes) and *Church Teaching on Human Sexuality* (7 minutes), and discuss the following questions:

1. Your children are growing up in a cultural context very different from the culture in which you grew up. Highlight and discuss several specific differences.

2. How did your parents protect you from the negative influences of the culture? How will you protect your children in similar or different ways?

3. List at least three ways you are trying to build a culture of pure love in your home.

4. *The Theology of the Body* teaches us that God has a plan for love and life. Describe God's plan as you understand it.

5. The author says in the video, "With our bodies, we can make God's invisible love visible . . . the sexual union within marriage expresses the fertile love of God." What difference would it make in our society if everyone truly believed that?

6. One of the parents, John, said he tells his boys that "only living things swim against the current and dead things flow with it." What does it mean to swim upstream? Name several specific actions you can take in your daily lives with your children to live out the meaning of this statement.

7. In the video, Arturo said, "I wish I had [this program] when I was growing up. I wish my dad would have taught me these things–I could have avoided so many problems." What problems do you hope to prevent for your children?

PART III

Watch the next two videos, *The First Stage of Love Learning: Early Childhood* (7 minutes) and *The Second Stage of Love Learning: Years of Innocence* (6 minutes), and discuss the following questions:

1. What are two ways you can teach little ones to have reverence for their bodies?

2. How can you begin to instill the tradition of our Faith into your children's lives? List some ways that you have seen to be successful.

3. Coleen mentions three virtues that should be taught to young children: obedience, generosity, and self-control. What is your experience in trying to teach these virtues? Mention the challenges you encounter in teaching these, and name some methods you can use to overcome those challenges.

4. How can we protect our children from pornography, even at these early stages?

5. Friendship begins to play an important role in the early grades of a child's life. What is the parent's role in helping children to develop good friendships?

6. Coleen suggests that children at this age can develop a personal relationship with Jesus. How can parents help this happen? Name at least three specific, daily actions you can take to instill this relationship.

PART IV

Watch the next two videos, *The Third Stage of Love Learning: Prepubescence* (6 minutes) and *The Fourth Stage of Love Learning: Adolescence* (9 minutes), and discuss the following questions:

1. This next part of the LoveEd program is designed to help parents teach their children about the changes that will happen during puberty and how they are a part of God's larger plan for marriage and family. What psychological and logistical hurdles can prevent parents from educating their children about these most important topics?

---

2. What things in the culture encourage children to grow up too soon? How can parents slow that down?

---

3. Coleen suggests that we teach our prepubescent children about chastity, which she defines as "the energy that helps us guide all our sexual attractions toward real love so that we know there is an important part of love that is only reserved for marriage." How would you teach that concept to ten-year-olds? To thirteen-year-olds?

---

4. Coleen says, "Teaching kids to avoid alcohol and drugs is as important to their moral education as it is to their personal and social education." Discuss what this means and how morality can be affected by drugs and alcohol.

_____

_____

_____

Continuing the Journey

Parents, you've come this far, don't quit now!

After reading the introduction to *LoveEd* and completing the Parent Training, take time to dig in to the substance of the issues that you will be facing as you raise your children. When questions arise, it's always helpful to have an understanding of the basic human principles upon which Church teachings are based. This will include age-appropriate biology and psychology, as well as the morality rooted both in science and in Scripture.

The following chapters of this book are designed to help you continue your journey. They're divided by the general age group of your child, yet each child is unique and will require answers according to their curiosity, maturity, and exposure to the media, as well as their outside experiences.

Once you've finished the Parent Training and read through the remainder of this book, you will have completed step one of this three-step process. Next comes the Parent/Child Events (at the appropriate ages you will complete Level 1 and Level 2 with your child) that open the door to better forms of communication. Following these events are the Parent/Child follow-up talks with reflection questions in the student guides, which can lead to ongoing conversation along their path of growth . . . and it can all be wonderful, not scary!

This journey in teaching love and relationships to your child will be amazing.

Imagine opening up his or her heart and mind to God's beautiful truth about love and sexuality, little by little.

Imagine being confident and prepared with a simple explanation of that truth when your child comes up with unexpected questions.

Imagine helping set the story straight when they're confused by someone's misinformation.

Most of all, imagine your child living out the truth and joy of relationships rooted in God's love, according to your guidance. That's the real benefit of these next *LoveEd* chapters for parents.

CHAPTER 1

God's Plan Written Within Our Bodies

I delight to do your will, my God;
your law is in my inner being!

—Psalm 40:9

God continues to enlighten us with the truths about ourselves through the sciences of biology, chemistry, physiology, and psychology. We also gain understanding through anthropology, sociology, human anatomy, bonding, emotions, and family life as revealed to us throughout human history.

God's plan for sexuality and morality is for our own good and protection. Deep down, written in our hearts, are all of the Ten Commandments, including "Thou shalt not kill," "Thou shalt not commit adultery," and "Thou shalt not covet thy neighbors' wife." It's up to us to live out that struggle between the flesh and the spirit while having confidence in the grace of God who sent His Son to redeem us from all sin.

However, blindness to the truth about man and woman exerts pressure to reduce sex to something commonplace and depersonalized. Therefore, our culture cannot adequately comprehend the real meaning of the gift of persons in marriage or celibacy, let alone responsible love at the service of fatherhood and motherhood and the true grandeur of procreation and education.[4]

The Church's Teaching on Human Sexuality

It helps to know the facts. The following pages reveal the beautiful truth of how the Church views sex and families. This section is written in bullet format to help you scan the material more easily and highlight certain passages that speak to you and your child's individual situation. Many of these bullets will be references from the *Catechism of the Catholic Church* (CCC), which is a book promulgated by Pope St. John Paul II in 1992. It serves as a summary of the beliefs of the Catholic faithful.

Human sexuality was a gift from the beginning of the creation of mankind (see Gn 1:27-28; 5:1-2).

- God designed our sexuality when He created us male and female. Our bodies are good and wonderful creations and can express the love of God. The differences between male and female are naturally ordered and good for us when they are lived according to God's design.
- God created us in His image—male and female—as complimentary sexes—genetically unique and different yet made for each other. God said, "man shall leave his father and mother, cling to his wife, and the two shall become one flesh" (see CCC 2331).
- God encouraged the man and woman to "be fruitful and multiply, fill the earth and subdue it," according to the plan He designed within our reproductive organs, our emotions, our intellect, and our ability to choose (see Gn 1:28).
- Our sexuality is part of a beautiful plan for happiness on heaven and earth; a reflection of God's total gift of love (see CCC 2332-33).
- The mutual gift of husband and wife in marriage is part of God's plan for humanity: it reflects the inner life of the Trinity—the love of the Father and Son comes alive in a whole new person, the Holy Spirit. And the love of a man and a woman comes alive in a whole new person whose soul will live for all eternity.
- It is a great privilege and responsibility to co-create new human life with God.

The theology of the body helps us understand our human nature and mission, along with God's grace and divine mercy.

- Developed throughout many years of anthropological study of humanity, and popularized by St. John Paul II in a series of homilies in his early papacy, the theology of the body helps explain the divine origin and natural beauty of our personhood, our inner desires, and our sexuality.
- Man and woman were made to complement and to care for each other; they are a gift to each other from God (see CCC 2334-35).
- Our bodies, our actions, and our relationships can make God's invisible love visible, seeing in each other the goodness of God. (For example, what does patience look like? Kindness? But when we *see* somebody being patient, God's love becomes visible.)
- In the beginning, when God created man and woman, they were in union with God and perfect harmony with one another. Praying was easy; communication between man and woman went well. They only saw the good in one another.
- Original sin, however, allowed the man and woman to see good *and* evil. It clouded their purity of vision, reducing the grace to see all good, thus inviting evil desires, too. This original sin changed the beautiful view into a distorted view, inviting man to lust and woman to manipulation, thus *using* instead of *loving* one another. Their relationships spiraled downward, and this distortion was passed on to their children and future generations.
- Even after God sent us the Ten Commandments as a covenant with Him, human beings struggled with their tendency to sin.

- So God sent His son, Jesus Christ, to save us. He came down to earth to free us to love and to show us what love looks like. He redeemed us from sin, offering the graces necessary to restore purity to all relationships, including and especially sexual relationships.

- While He was here on earth teaching us how to love and live, Jesus even challenged us to purity of our thoughts—He said we shouldn't even look at a woman with lust or we are committing adultery in our heart (see Mt 5:27-28). Jesus also said, "Blessed are the clean of heart, for they will see God" (Mt 5:8).

- Jesus looked at all men and women with great mercy, continually offering His healing grace to absolve them of their sins and start again. "Neither do I condemn you. Go, [and] from now on do not sin any more," He told the woman caught in adultery (Jn 8:11).

- As Christians, we are called to show the world what the love of God looks like. He gives us the grace and mercy through the sacraments to do so.

Sexual morality teaches us about the meaning of the marriage act.

- God's desire is that each married couple will have the best love experience possible—a reflection of His love that is faithful and open to new life.

- A man and a woman enter into the Sacrament of Matrimony to publicly proclaim their loving lifetime commitment and ask God's blessing and graces for their newly formed family. A lifetime of joys, struggles, and sacrifices offer couples opportunities to grow deeper in love and closer to God through this vocation of marriage.

- The conjugal union is a consummation of and continued renewal of the marriage covenant, a sign of the Sacrament of Matrimony. The marriage act continues to bond the couple in a personal, chemical, spiritual, and physical way during the years of marriage, renewing God's grace with the renewing of the vows. This union must always be open to the possibility of new life born of this loving union so that their love will be fruitful forever (see CCC 2360-65).

- All sexually pleasurable activity belongs in marriage as a preparation for, and culminating in, the conjugal union of husband and wife.

- Masturbation, whether single or mutual, is an offense against the dignity and purpose of sexual pleasure and the marriage act and is "gravely disordered" (CCC 2352).

- Sexual activity outside of marriage is immoral; this includes fornication, such as premarital sex, adultery, or extramarital sex. The body language is dishonest—it says, "I give my whole self. . . . Oh, no, I don't!"

- This conjugal act can only take place between a man and a woman due to the fact that their anatomy has the opposite sexual organs to become "one flesh." Introducing the reproductive system to the digestive system is not a conjugal marriage act, whether attempted inside or outside of marriage. Thus, such acts are not a sexual union, but merely the use of the sexual organs for a false and gravely disordered purpose.

- The sexual union, conception, and childbearing belong within marriage. "The origin of human life has its authentic context in marriage and in the family, where it is generated through an act which expresses the reciprocal love between a man and a woman. In procreation that is truly responsible, the child to be born 'must be the fruit of marriage.'"[5]

- Couples who discover they are sterile suffer greatly, yet they must use only the morally acceptable means of fertility enhancement that do not separate the conjugal act from the procreation of the child. This is out of respect for the dignity of the child.
- Each conjugal act must be fully human, not just based on instincts. Each act must take place within a loving, faithful marriage and be open to the possibility of life.

The body language of the conjugal (marriage) act means openness to life and love.

- The marriage act, which is an intimate and chaste union of spouses, is noble and honorable. It enriches the spouses in joy, pleasure, and gratitude (see CCC 2362).
- The spouses' union achieves the twofold end of marriage: the good of the spouses themselves and the transmission of life. These two meanings cannot be separated without altering the couple's spiritual life and compromising the goods of marriage and the future of the family (see CCC 2663). Thus, conjugal love is obligated to be both faithful and open to life.
- All family planning is to be responsible and done in accord with the natural rhythms of the body. Married couples are invited to learn the daily signs that God reveals through the woman's body that indicate her daily level of fertility.
- If for serious reasons a married couple thinks it would be irresponsible to conceive a child that month, they abstain from the conjugal union during the five to seven days of fertility in that cycle, thus respecting the true meaning of the marriage act.[6]
- Using only natural methods allows couples to maintain the integrity of the meaning of the marriage act as God created it; the act of conjugal union always says, "I give myself totally to you, unconditionally and forever."
- Contraception and sterilization not only harm the body but put conditions on love, thus avoiding the "total self-gift" of one to the beloved, reducing the union to pleasure seeking. This attempt to split the inseparable qualities of the love-giving and life-giving bond of the marriage act can harm the emotional, psychological, and spiritual unity of the marriage.
- Using Natural Family Planning requires a deep love and commitment which one should already have with one's spouse and also requires the self-discipline and virtue necessary to consider the needs of the spouse, the family, and society.
- Marital chastity is the virtue that helps us live out God's natural plan for our family of being faithful and open to life.

Chastity is a virtue that helps us live our sexuality according to God's design.

- Chastity is a virtue that directs our sexual desires toward a pure and real love and keeps us from using people as objects for our own selfish pleasure.
- Chastity is the virtue of sexual purity. Outside of marriage, chastity includes abstinence. Inside of marriage, it includes faithfulness and openness to life.
- Chastity keeps love honest, personal, selfless, and faithful. In this world of superficiality, chastity makes love *real*.
- Chastity grows on the building blocks of all the other virtues: self-control, honesty, courage, faithfulness, patience, kindness.

- Chastity helps lead to physical, mental, social, and spiritual health.
- Chastity provides freedom to grow in maturity, individuality, and self-respect.
- Chastity helps people in romantic relationships develop better friendships.
- The commitment to chastity gives young people the freedom to make better choices about life, free from the emotional, psychological, physical, and chemical bondage of sexual sin.

Chastity leads to self-mastery.

- Chastity is an apprenticeship in self-mastery, which is training in human freedom.
- The alternative is clear: Either we govern our passions and find peace or we let ourselves be dominated by them and become unhappy (see CCC 2339).
- Chastity includes avoiding occasions that might provoke or encourage sin as well as knowing how to overcome one's own natural instinctive impulses.
- Chastity makes the personality harmonious. It matures it and fills it with inner peace.
- Chastity strengthens our character, helping us to learn true love.

Chastity leads to joy.

- Chastity is the joyous affirmation of someone who knows how to live a life of self-giving, free from any form of self-centered slavery.
- This presupposes that the person has learned how to accept other people, to relate with them while respecting their dignity in diversity.
- The chaste person is not self-centered, not involved in selfish relationships with other people.
- Chastity makes the personality harmonious. It matures it and fills it with inner peace.[7]

Cultural Confusion About Human Sexuality

Due to the confusion and lies of this age, we need to teach our children the basic truths very clearly, gradually, and sensitively at the proper times of life. We live in a culture that does not form our children in the truth—rather, it "deforms" them and causes distortion and confusion. The results are rampant offenses against the dignity of the person. People use others as objects for pleasure, money, entertainment, or control. People often treat their own bodies and their relationships as disposable. In the past, even if parents did not provide a specific education in human sexuality, the general culture respected, supported, and protected the dignity of the human person. This is not true in today's culture, where distorted sexual messages are everywhere.

Therefore, if you are not talking to your kids about sex, someone else is!

The Disordered Use of Sex

Our modern culture paints a warped picture of sex. This disordered use of sex can:

- Destroy a person's capacity to love by making pleasure (instead of sincere self-giving) the goal of sexuality.[8]

- Make pleasure the *goal* of sexuality, rather than the *gift*.
- Reduce other persons to objects of gratification and develop habits of using others rather than giving of ourselves.
- Harm one's ability to love or give of oneself in marriage or in any relationship.

Aware of the dangers of our modern culture, parents want to understand the evils they need to alert their children to in order to protect them. The parent discerns the right timing to share appropriate information to be equipped as Christ's disciples and protected from activities that violate their personal dignity and that of others. It's important that parents understand these issues first in order to form their children in them.

The Church lifts up the dignity of the person; while disordered use of sex does not. In varying degrees of gravity, the teachings on the violations of chastity[9] include:

- **Immodest behavior and dress, or indecent speech,** that is contrary to the God-given dignity of the person and leads others away from authentic love.
- **Misuse of the Internet or other electronic devices**, such as cell phones, for viewing or posting sexually explicit material.
- **Pornography and indecent entertainment** that injure the dignity of the viewer and denigrate the intimacy of the marital act.
- **Risky behaviors**, such as the abuse of alcohol or drugs, that often lead to lower inhibitions, increasing the risk of regretted sexual encounters.
- **Masturbation,** a disordered act that creates a harmful and often lifelong habit of selfishness.
- **Artificial contraception** that separates the life-giving/love-giving bond from sexual intercourse. (This is a commonly misunderstood topic, but the good news is that the healthy and effective alternative called Natural Family Planning actually improves marital bonding and communication.)
- **Use of reproductive technologies** violates the dignity of the person and of the marriage act through which each child is designed to come into the world. This puts the doctor in control instead of God, and often results in multiple conceived children, many of whom are then "discarded" in the laboratory.
- **Premarital sex**, including oral sex and mutual masturbation, which are forms of fornication. Although contrary to popular opinion today, purity and faithfulness are what Jesus commands us for our own greater good.
- **Cohabitation** and civil unions that contain sexual activity cheat a couple from creating the proper environment for the relationship to grow in love and form a stable home for a family.
- **Homosexual acts** contrary to chastity use the body in ways for which it was not designed. They are also outside of the definition of marriage, which is between one man and one woman.
- **Adultery and polygamy,** which are directly opposed to the faithful and exclusive lifelong union between one man and one woman.

- **Prostitution,** the degrading use of the sexual powers that harms the dignity of the person by using others' bodies as objects for pleasure or financial gain.
- **Rape, incest, and sexual abuse,** criminal acts that violate God's law and the health and dignity of the person.

The above list is not meant to provide children with information they are not ready for, nor does it mean that you give them overly explicit answers. Rather, in a gradual way, help your child understand how these sexual sins are outside of God's plan. Some examples of how to relay sensitive, age-appropriate information to children are included in the parent chapters for each age group.

Answering one question at a time, with age-appropriate information, allows parents to reveal the goodness of God's plan for men and women and marriage. The graces you receive in the sacrament of marriage will help you on this journey.

It's evident that many parts of our Catholic moral code are unpopular today. It's easy to write off these issues as just being "what people do." There also needs to be compassion for those who haven't been formed with a Catholic moral code and aren't aware of the inherent dangers and negative effects of these issues. All of us struggle and fail at different behaviors, even if we do know what is right and wrong. God's forgiveness is the key to growing closer to Him in love. His mercy gives us the wisdom and strength to live love well. The Church is here to help us and guide us to live the best love, God's love.

Since sexual sin is popular in many cultures, it helps to take the time to study some of the issues until we understand the beautiful reasons behind the Church's directions. There is wisdom behind each of the Church's teachings. As we grow to understand them and obey them, we will gain that wisdom as well. You can learn more by reading the section on the Catechism about the sixth commandment, or by talking to a parish leader who understands and lives out these beautiful teachings.

God Gives Married Couples the Grace to Live and Love Well: The World Needs It

Real love is possible in any and all circumstances thanks to the grace of God. The witness of Christian love is desperately needed in our world today. Our brokenness due to original sin can lead us to discord and even discouragement. God, knowing this, sent His Son to save us. Jesus also instituted the Sacrament of Matrimony, by which married couples can regularly receive the graces they need to live out their vocation to marriage and family. Think of God's love as a spiritual bank account that never empties, as long as we use the correct password. God's love is without limits.

Some Catholic concepts that help us live this love well include:

- We are created in the image and likeness of God. This is our nature.
- To be free, we must love like God does, reflecting His love to others.
- God's love is always life-giving. In God, life and love are part of the same gift.
- To live in freedom, in the dignity of our human nature, married love must also be inseparably life-giving and love-giving.

- In God's plan, love and life-giving are both unconditional and forever.
- As witnesses to God's unconditional love, you make the world a better place.

Contemporary society has a special need of the witness of couples who persevere in their union as an eloquent, even if sometimes suffering, "sign" in our human condition of the steadfastness of God's love.[10] So as married couples, you become a sign to others of Christ's love.

Strong, Smart, and Pure: For Parents ⟶ Rewind

Strong: You now have the strength of knowledge and commitment of the Church to help your family fight the dysfunctional messages of the culture.

Smart: You now understand the basis of God's beautiful intent for marriage and sexuality as taught from Scripture, the Church, and within our bodies.

Pure: You and your family are now ready to implement the ways you can choose purity and chastity as the ways God wants us to live.

Strong, Smart, and Pure: Fast Forward ⟶ Into Your Home

Strong: You will learn how to be strong in leading your family on the path toward real love and virtue; how to establish your house as a place of family well-being and peace; and you will be the first to set the good example.

Smart: You will see how to teach from the perspective of love—to show your children how to live the virtues, find their first resources in you and in living their faith, and have the right perspective when it comes to media usage, self-image, and interacting with others. You will also learn what and when specific topics should be discussed through "teachable moments."

Pure: Living pure love in our growing family can include working together, praying together, and playing together.

CHAPTER 2

Teaching Sexuality Within the Context of Love

Basically, education for authentic love, is authentic only if it becomes kind, well-disposed love, involves accepting the person who is loved and considering his or her good as one's own; hence this implies educating in right relationships with others.

—Pontifical Council for the Family, The Truth and Meaning of Human Sexuality, n. 53

Parents, you can do this job best. Have confidence and prepare yourself for it. You know your child and his or her unique personality. You can often sense your child's timing and need for information. You are present for your child. You realize what your child needs to know and when. You can discern your child's thoughts and attitudes.

And in everyday situations, you can teach your child what his or her body is for. Many times we need to remind our children what they are here for: "Your job as a person is to *love* your brothers and sisters. You can use your voice, your eyes, your hands, and your feet to love them. You can do favors for them, you can hug them, and you can speak to them with kindness and patience. That's your job as a family member—to love one another."

Family Love and Bonding: Building an Atmosphere of Family Joy and Unity

Parents are called to create an atmosphere of Christian joy in their homes. This joy in Christ can carry you through all the trials you will face. In turn, your children will learn by your example. Adapting gospel values, a family lovingly nurtures, instructs, and affirms the good in each family member. This is a challenge when life becomes too busy and overtaxing, or during periods of great suffering. These are times when we must turn to God in prayer with even greater fervor. The family can and should become your place of prayer, peace, and respite, like an oasis from the worldly concerns. Disagreements or arguments should always work toward positive resolutions, not as food for wounded egos. Downtime and togetherness help create family bonds that can withstand the storms of life. If you do not take the time to build a strong family, it will not just happen on its own.

How do we continue to bond our family together in love when life gets busy or difficult?

First, we need to spend time on activities that can touch the heart and create good memories. Rooted in love, a family in this age of technology should make a concerted effort to **work together, play together, and pray together**.

Work Together. To grow a strong and intimate family, it is essential that you develop teamwork. This begins with the parents working as a team on various projects and extends as the children grow. Some opportunities are family chores, projects for the home, neighborhood, or school, cooking together, cleaning up meals together, and even working together to get rid of things you can bring to the poor.

Play Together. When do we create this atmosphere of joy and unity amidst our busy work lives, sports, food preparation, commuting, etc.? If we barely have time for ourselves, how are we going to have time for our children? Remember to have fun together so that children remember more than your instructions, discipline, and corrections.

Family "down time" used to be an ordinary part of life, but now it is something that must be scheduled in and planned. But it's worth scheduling!

These opportunities should take priority while building a strong, united family:

- Family dinners each night
- A peaceful bedtime for the children
- Weekly family fun hour to break up the stress of the week
- Sundays for relaxation with God and nature
- Monthly dates for Mom and Dad to strengthen their relationship while having fun
- Vacations with your immediate family

Family time provides some of the best opportunities to teach the virtues of respect, sharing, obedience, patience, forgiveness, gratitude, and helpfulness. That way the virtues are not always taught when correcting or scolding, but can be developed and practiced in normal family life.

Pray together. Bless each member of your family each morning and offer your day to God. Bless them again each night before bed. Pray and bless your meals and snacks. Our good example leads our children to heaven as we pray with them and live a life of virtue. Each parent should take the personal responsibility to grow in love and grace, embracing the virtues of faith, hope, love, prudence, justice, fortitude, and temperance.

A parent's good example begins by taking the children to weekly Mass, praying together as a family each day, keeping the Ten Commandments, and living the moral virtues in daily life.

The Ten Commandments are not just a stone tablet Moses brought down the mountain from God but rather the beginning of a framework for a civilized and dignified society and family life. The Ten Commandments were given to us by God, who loves us with a passion and wants us to live our lives in peace and harmony. No matter what situations we face within our families, we should always strive to live the commandments and challenge one another to do so. Teaching them to your children can become a normal part of your examination of conscience during evening prayer.

Atmosphere in the Home for Teaching Chastity

Building family love through daily time and activities provides many opportunities to live out our faith. A child who feels secure and loved at home has a better chance to develop healthy relationships outside the home. An atmosphere of love in your home is more conducive to teaching the virtue of chastity to your children. There are a number of ways we can create this atmosphere, even years before our children learn about the word chastity.

- Make your home a peaceful place, always working toward harmony and valuing good relationships. Don't complain about your spouse to your children or let them hear you criticize your spouse to others.
- Create a home of faith and prayer where God's presence and love are felt.
- Tell your children you love them many times a day, have fun together, and practice Christian joy!
- Build up the virtues of charity, temperance, and fortitude. Charity is opening your children's hearts to kindness in words and deeds—first with their siblings and then in service to others as they mature. Temperance is practicing balance in all things, such as getting enough sleep, proper nutrition, cleanliness, and orderliness. Fortitude is the courage to do the right thing no matter what the consequences.
- Spend downtime together to foster closeness. Be conscious of how you spend your Sundays. Relax together and appreciate God and His creation.
- Be generous in accepting new life into the family; be open to having more children when you can. Build a community of love so your children will learn love at all stages of life. This calls for sacrifice, and it naturally helps fight individualism, consumerism, and selfishness.
- Adapt a simpler lifestyle so family love becomes more important than having "stuff."
- Teach your children how to develop healthy relationships with God, their siblings, and their companions. Pray together, work together, and play together.
- Teach your children to make sacrifices for love of God and for the good of others. Their free wills must be continually trained to embrace the little "crosses" of the day without complaining.
- Discipline your children for maturity and moral strength. A spoiled child used to getting his own way is not predisposed to real love or chastity. Train them in selflessness rather than selfishness; it will be the basis of their success in a future marriage.
- Parents must ensure a moderate, critical, watchful, and prudent use of media. Teach your children how to avoid and resist the distortions of love depicted in the movies, TV shows, and music. Open their minds to great literature, stories of the saints, and great people who made a difference for goodness with their lives.
- Teach self-control in all areas of your children's lives. Model how to live in an orderly way, respecting themselves and others. Teach peer-pressure resistance and help them know

you are there to support them in doing good, even if they feel alone in their choices with their peers.

How Parents Can Gain the Confidence They Need to Teach Chastity

Here are some of the fundamentals of teaching chastity to your children:

- Pray for guidance from God, pray for your children, and pray for their future spouse.
- Show love and affection in your home. Many teens go out to find the love they desire and wrongly substitute a sexual relationship for their unmet need for family love.
- Know and live Church teachings regarding chastity within and outside of marriage. Be loving and faithful to your spouse, offer your love and kindness to your husband or wife each day, and practice natural family planning so you can experience the fullness of God's graces of matrimony and the unity with one another.
- Single parents should be good examples of purity, modesty, and chastity, whether or not they are dating. They should speak respectfully of marriage and the child's other parent; out of respect for your children, be careful not to create division.
- Regular confession offers us God's mercy, healing, and confidence so we do not have to pass on our old baggage or sexual hang-ups to our children. God wants to free us from our past through the confessional. Take advantage of His goodness and mercy.
- The Eucharist brings us the strength we need when we are up against a culture that does not know God's love. Stay full of God's grace. Never miss Sunday Mass!
- Practice real love and concern for your children's souls, not just their bodies.
- Avoid pornography and indecent entertainment, protecting both you and your children from its deadening effects.
- Learn more about sexual morality; study the theology of the body. Grow in your understanding of what it means to be a gift of love to others.
- Learn more about your Catholic faith by reading the Gospels and the *Catechism*.

Parent Check-up!

How many of the following are currently happening in your home? Check all that apply to reveal areas where your family is excelling and where improvement is needed. Be encouraged that no parents are perfect as we deal with the many demands of daily life. Congratulate yourself for the progress you are making. This checklist will help direct you along the path to even greater growth!

- ☐ We touch the heart by personally sharing quality time with our child as we discuss the mysteries of life.
- ☐ We provide an understanding of the reasoning behind Church teachings.
- ☐ We promote the fruit of grace and good habits, enriched by the sacraments.
- ☐ Formation is experienced in the family with the example of the parent(s).
- ☐ We are rooted and sustained in prayer.
- ☐ We teach how to avoid near occasions of sin.
- ☐ We include supportive catechesis in virtue from the parish and school.

☐ We teach by example of virtues.

☐ Our lines of communication are open.

☐ We give clear directions and discipline.

☐ We encourage, support, and speak often with other faithful parents.

☐ Education in love is expressed in awe of God's creation and handiwork.

Guiding principles in education for love within the family that should be used in each stage of a child's life:[11]

- Each child is a unique and unrepeatable person and must receive individualized formation. *A very curious, inquisitive child may ask more questions sooner than others. Quiet children may need you to bring up the topic at an appropriate time.*

- The moral dimension must always be part of the parent's explanation. *Explain how God created us and God's plan for all people to follow His directions for their own good and the good of others.*

- Formation and information must be provided in the broadest context of education for love. *Information outside of the beauty of God's plan for love, marriage, and family, or scientific information that is given too early, can keep children from properly integrating the moral information.*

- Parents should provide this information with great sensitivity but clearly and at the appropriate time. *Pray to know what God is asking of you as you speak to each child. Listen more than talk if you want to find out what impressions they have or what they already know.*

The working principles of education for sexuality include four important topics: doctrine, timing, decency, and respect:[12]

- Doctrine
  - Catholic Doctrine and Morals should always be followed, educating in accordance with God, who is Love.
  - Respect the sacred mystery and dignity of the person teaching that chastity is possible and brings joy to one's life.
  - Be aware of the temptations due to the effects of original sin.
- Timing
  - Only give information proportionate to the child's development.
  - Respect their innocence and psychological growth.
- Decency
  - Decency should be used in speech, action, and dress.
  - No erotic material should be shown to children.
- Respect
  - Offend no one's modesty, delicacy, or privacy.
  - Speak respectfully of persons and God's plan for sexuality.

Parents are also welcome to seek the assistance of the Church in these matters of education for love, but the Church cannot do this task for you. The Church does not want to take the role of sex education from the parent because it respects the privacy of the topic, as well as keeping it in the context of education for love. Thus, Church support for education in love has its limitations as stated by the United States bishops. The intimate details of biology or emotions and private questions that take place in the family can be supplemented by the supportive catechesis of the local parish or school.

Learning Stages for Human Sexuality Education in the Context of Love

There are five stages of learning about human sexuality, and they are best addressed in a gradual way throughout the years. Keeping in mind that each child should receive individualized formation, parents can adapt these to the child.

- **Young Children**–Birth to Age Six
- **Age of Innocence**–Age Five to Puberty
- **Puberty**–Preparation for Changes from Child to Adult
- **Early Adolescence**–Young Teens During or After Puberty
- **Adolescence Toward Adulthood**–High School and Early College Years

Strong, Smart, and Pure: Education for Love ⟹ Rewind

Strong: Your strength of virtue will lead your family through life. You will set the example on how to live a rightly ordered life, and you will make your house a place of peace where your children can feel comfortable discussing every aspect of life with you.

Smart: You will teach your children how to live the virtues, how to discuss with you (rather than their peers or the culture) the things they need to know, including the importance of living their faith. You will teach them how to manage themselves and not be led by inappropriate feelings or actions.

Pure: It's worth repeating: the family that works together, plays together, and prays together can live pure lives together.

Strong, Smart, and Pure: Fast Forward ⟹ For Very Young Children:

Strong: From infants through the age of six, children need your strength physically: changing their diapers, feeding them, developing a daily schedule for them, and playing with them. As they grow through this period, your strength will be challenged as you learn the need for patience in teaching them age-appropriate behaviors. The guidance of the Church can help you.

Smart: You will be given the confidence and processes by which you can address your children's behaviors and questions. "What is this called?" "Why shouldn't I do that?" "Where do babies come from?" How should these types of questions be addressed?

Pure: Each child is pure and full of grace at their baptism. Your children have clean souls, and they can begin to learn truth and proper behaviors right from the beginning. Keeping them pure is a reachable goal!

CHAPTER 3

LoveEd for Your Child from Birth to Age Six

*No one is capable of giving moral
education regarding human sexuality
better than duly prepared parents.*

—Pope St. John Paul II,
The Family in the Modern World

From the moment your child is known to be in the womb, you are teaching him or her about love and sexuality. Parents have always known by instinct what the latest technology has confirmed: A child in the womb can feel pain, hear you sing and talk, feel your love, and absorb your emotions and attitudes. At birth, this education continues. The child knows the difference between Dad's scratchy beard and Mom's long hair. A new baby knows which parent has the milk he or she requires to survive and instinctually finds it. The breastfeeding mother is in a natural position for cuddling and embracing the child on a very regular basis. Mothers who do not breastfeed need to know the importance of embracing and skin contact, keeping the child close to their heart.

Adopted children are just as warmly welcomed into the family, "chosen" by the parents and by God to be part of this family. While you have little control over their experience in the womb, they can sense and experience your excitement and love, giving them a beautiful sense of belonging to your family community of love. The way we treat our children is the beginning of our *LoveEd*.

Babies can sense that Dad's approach to holding them is different than Mom's. Education in sexuality has begun. Children first learn about masculinity and femininity from their mothers and fathers by the way they are carried, handled, and treated. They hear the rougher voice of Dad and the softer voice of Mom. This is all part of God's plan for men, women, and children. They also notice how their parents love one another. Your child's education in marriage begins with his or her observations of you.

Your respect for your children's bodies is shown by the way you change their diapers, dress or undress them, and bathe them. The way you touch them and treat them teaches them how to treat their own bodies and how to treat others. Can you imagine absorbing all of this education before you can even talk? God made us amazing!

During this young age, a child has very little modesty or shame. Running naked around the house is not unusual or wrong, but may need to be reined in when company is present. Young children are discovering their identity and learning to control their hands, their bathroom habits, their language, their emotions, their temper, and their place in the family. They normally associate closely with their mother from the womb, growing into a relationship with their father as he cares for them and loves them.

Name the Private Parts

Just as you teach your children to name the other parts of their bodies, teach them the proper names of their sexual organs. This often occurs when they are learning other words as toddlers, whether while getting dressed or taking a bath.

If you're not yet comfortable using the proper names, or you used slang names as a child or with your child up until this point, it would be helpful to practice the proper anatomical names until they become more natural to you.

A conversation might go like this:

> "Joey, that is called your penis. It is just for boys. Daddy has a penis, too."
> "Don't you have a penis, Mommy?"
> "No, mommies and girls have different private parts than boys."
> "Why don't you have a penis, Mommy?"
> "Mommy doesn't need a penis. God made her different than boys. I am a woman. My private parts are called the labia and vagina. That's one way God made us to be different; He made us male and female, boys or girls."
> "Can I see it, Mommy?"
> "No, it is a private part, and we don't show our private parts to anyone, remember?"
> "Oh, yeah, I always remember that my private parts should be private, too, mommy.

Joey may start repeating the words, as toddlers often do. "Mommy has a 'gina. Joey has a penis." This gives you a chance for further instruction.

> "Joey, I want you to know the proper names for the private parts, but remember that they are private, so we don't talk about them when other people are around, okay?"

When toddlers take off their clothes at inappropriate times, remind them:

> "Joey, we should always keep our private parts covered."

If you catch them playing with themselves in the bathtub, say:

> "Joey, we are not supposed to play with or rub our private parts, but we do

need to keep them clean. So let's wash them now so we can get out of the tub and get dried off and dressed. We should always keep our private parts covered with our underwear, and we shouldn't put our hands down there either."

Note how a redirection to wash up here helps.

The Curiosity of Toddlers

Preschoolers are curious about everything, including their bodies. Don't be alarmed if they have questions about their private parts, or yours. Your daughter may ask:

"Mommy, why does Joey have a penis and I don't? I have nothing!"

You can answer:

"Because God made us to be girls, and we have a vagina inside of us, not a penis on the outside. That's one way that God made men different than women."
"Is this my vagina?"
"No, those folds of skin are called labia. It is kind of a funny word we don't hear much. We wash our labia in the bathtub, and dry it well, too, before we put our underwear on."
"Where is my vagina then?"
"The labia are those folds of skin that protect the opening to your vagina, which is inside."

Too many details too early can confuse them, so keep your answers simple.

Provide Simple Correct Facts About Sexuality, but Not Explicit Details

Simple information about pregnancy and the birth of a brother or sister can be taught to very young children.
A conversation might sound like this:

"Guess what? Our family is going to have another baby!"
"Where is it, Mommy?"
"Our new baby is very tiny right now and is growing in mommy's womb."
"Where's that, Mommy?"
"It's a special place God made right under mommy's heart. When the baby gets bigger, we will be able to feel it move around inside of me. You know when we say the Hail Mary, we say, 'Blessed is the fruit of your womb'? Every baby, even Jesus, grows in their mother's womb. God made us in an awesome way, and we are excited that we are going to have a new baby."

Make sure to use the term "womb" and not "tummy" as your child might confuse this with the bodily functions of digestion.

If the question comes up of how the baby got in there, a simple answer for this age could be:

> "God has a special way of starting the baby to grow inside of a mom when the mom and dad love each other very much."

You can add to this later.

In a few years, when children are five or six, additional questions may arise regarding pregnancy.

> "Jessica, we have some good news—we're going to have another baby!"
> "Oh . . . will it cry all the time like Sarah did when she was a baby?"
> "We don't know, but Daddy and I know that we will all try to love this baby like we did you and Sarah. You can help us love her and take care of her, too."
> "Will you still love me, Mommy?"
> "Of course I will, Jess! Now the love in our family will grow even more, since we have more people to love."

After Jessica has time to think about it for a few days, she may ask more questions.

> "Mom, how do you know there is a baby in there? You don't have a big belly."
> "There is a urine test you can get at the doctor's office or buy at the drugstore that lets you know if your body shows signs that a baby is living inside you."
> "When will you get a big belly?"
> "In a few months when the baby grows bigger, the muscles in my uterus will stretch and grow around the baby. Then I will have a big belly."
> "How does the baby get in there?"
> "God has a special way for husbands and wives to love each other with a special holy hug. They get so close together that Daddy can plant the seeds of life inside of Mom's body. Then we pray and ask God to bless us with a new baby, and sometimes He does."
> "How does the baby get out of there?"
> "Remember that special private opening called the vagina that only girls have? It has another name called the birth canal. When the baby is fully grown and ready to be born, the vagina stretches open and God helps the baby move through it to the outside of the body."
> "Does it hurt when the baby comes out, Mommy?"
> "It does for a while as the muscles push the baby out, but after you see your beautiful little baby, you forget that it hurt and are happy that you have a new baby. Many moms go to the hospital to have their baby, and the doctors and nurses can give the mom medicine and help the mom and baby during the birth."
> "Birth? Is that why we call our birthday a *birthday*?"
> "Exactly! We are so happy that you were born that we celebrate you every year on that day! Let's say a prayer right now to thank God that you were born!"

Toddler Masturbation

A delicate but common issue during this stage is toddler masturbation. Small children have a tendency to experiment with every part of their bodies. Although it is common, the habit does not go away on its own if the child is allowed to regularly stimulate the pleasure center of their brain in this way. It is not a sin for them yet but rather a discovery that needs to be redirected until it is no longer a habit.

Tell the child not to rub their private parts. Tell them it is wrong and suggest something else to do whenever they feel like doing that. Some alternatives that provide comfort might be rocking a special doll in the rocking chair, rubbing their teddy bear's back, or hugging their dolls. Quite often, due to the sensual nature of masturbation, a child just needs to get up and be more active by doing jumping jacks or hitting a punching bag to release any pent-up energy.

Many parents have found that the change of activity or energy level is enough. Others find that redirection sends the child into hiding under the bed or under the covers to experience the sensations they seek. If this is the case, redirection may not be enough. Be loving and firm, but not harsh. The child may be expressing the need for additional hugging, holding, or parental affection. Your little one might need to do something fun, physical, and exciting with you, such as running around the house, playing tag, wrestling or tickling, or dancing to their favorite music. Physically fun alternatives can create an enjoyable substitute for the body and the soul, as well as providing some laughter and smiles that every family needs anyway.

The challenge for parents is that while masturbation is disordered, it is not abnormal for children just discovering themselves and their sensations. Masturbation is a more difficult habit to break as a child gets older. For the sake of your children's sexual maturity, it is good to redirect them and stop it now. Many experts who misadvise about this do not understand the full meaning of self-gift in the theology of the body. Secular sex educators will probably tell you to just let your child masturbate in private. But that bad advice will hinder your child's sexual development toward becoming an "other-centered," loving person. Masturbation is the opposite of self-gift, and it is a misuse of the sexual pleasure center, which leads to the common but erroneous acceptance of eroticism for its own sake as normal. That secular view of selfish sexual pleasure is against all Christian principles of love.

So how do we teach that to a small child? This would be time for some moral guidance.

> "No, Janie, we are not supposed to touch ourselves there."
> "But I just feel funny inside when I do it, and I like it."
> "That's not what your private parts or your hands are for, Janie. What is something good you can do with your body?"
> "But I want to."
> "We must find something else that you want to do whenever you feel like doing that. What would be fun for you?"
> "Can I sing my favorite song in the house?"
> "Yes, that's better, except when the baby is sleeping."
> "What can I do when the baby is sleeping?"
> "How about if you jump on the mini-trampoline downstairs? That's a better way to use your energy."

"You mean I can jump on the mini-trampoline every day if I want?"

"Yes, Janie, that is a good use of your energy, so let's remember that together."

"Okay, Mommy."

Teach Safety from Predators

As children move out from their family circle into other circles of life, they need additional instructions. Part of teaching our children to love is teaching them what love is *not*. Some love relationships can be damaged and repaired, but others are seriously harmful and need to be avoided totally. Help them see that some relationships are positive and loving, such as playing with Grandma or a certain family friend. Other relationships can be harmful or destructive, such as they see on the cartoons or movies that show "good and evil" or bad guys and good guys. Due to the evil in the world, not every person or action is loving. There are bad actions our children need to be warned to avoid. Sometimes someone they know may try to do something to harm them.

Offer gentle instruction for safety from predators. Tell them:

> "Never let anyone look at or touch your private parts, even if they ask you. Not your friends, or brothers or sisters, uncles or aunts, or anybody. Only Mommy or Daddy may help you when you are bathing or dressing, or the doctor may need to examine you when you are at his office. No one else may take pictures of your private parts, either. If someone touches you in a private place, say no to them in a loud voice. Yell and get away from that person, and come tell us or get help from a grown-up. Don't keep something like that a secret."

As your child gets older and spends more time away from home, additional instructions for boundaries and safety should be delicately taught. We do not want our children to fear affection, but we do want them to have a healthy avoidance of inappropriate touching.

Practice These Virtues for Early Education in Love

These first six years of childhood are the time to teach the basic virtues of obedience, generosity, and self-control. Help your child practice, step-by-step, how to say no to what is bad and yes to what is good. These basic virtues lay the foundation for a lifetime of virtue.

Obedience means your child should promptly, cheerfully do what he or she is told. It may include helping you around the house, putting his or her clothes in the laundry, or turning off the television when it's time for bed. Training in loving obedience now can help your child learn to live for others instead of his or her own feelings. The practice of loving obedience helps form the basis of other virtues. Cheerful, prompt obedience without selfishness can also prevent the eye-rolling that often comes with entering adolescence.

Generosity is a challenging virtue to teach toddlers, who often identify with their belongings. Sharing a toy might take some practice; doing something nice for their sibling may or may not come naturally. Young children can learn to give by sharing a song they learned or by putting part of their allowance in the church collection basket.

Self-control is developed over time during these ages of one to seven, so persevere, parents! Patiently show little ones that a greater good will come through a small sacrifice now: "Clean up your coloring, and then we can go to the park"; or "We are not going to touch this birthday cake yet so that later everyone at the party will enjoy this beautiful cake together."

A child who does not learn to obey his or her parents will have a difficult time obeying God. A child who does not learn to be generous can grow up to be stingy in personal matters, too, and be quite challenged when it comes to giving himself or herself unconditionally in marriage. A child who does not learn self-control will not automatically have sexual self-control when it comes to chastity or purity. This is how the virtues become the foundation of a strong, smart, and pure life through adolescence and adulthood.

Ten Tips for Parents of Young Children Using Teachable Moments About Love and Life

1. Have confidence in God's grace—this was all His idea anyway.
2. Try not to overreact when a question arises, and listen carefully to what your child is saying.
3. Do not laugh or make fun of your child's question.
4. Find a separate, quiet place for private discussions.
5. It's okay to say, "I don't know" if your children ask you something you are not prepared to answer. But let them know you will find out, and bring it up again soon.
6. Be honest, but give partial answers that a child can handle.
7. Ask your child to clarify what you have taught so you know he or she has heard the information correctly.
8. Always share moral teachings rooted in God's plan and ask your child for his or her assent to that plan.
9. Discussions with father and mother together is the best approach for ongoing education during puberty and adolescence.
10. Pray together when you are finished discussing these topics, allowing God to bless your child and your teaching.

Games for Parents with Their Children to Reinforce Concepts

It's always good and healthy to play some good, old-fashioned games with your children. Not only does this create wonderful memories of happy times, but these games will help teach obedience and self-discipline in a fun way.

Here are some examples:
- Red Light, Green Light
- Mother, May I?
- Simon Says

Strong, Smart, and Pure: For Ages 1-6 ⟹ Rewind

Strong: Trust that God's love for you and your child will help you to be strong at this physically challenging—but most joyful!—time of life. Enjoy the journey: the smiles, the messy diapers, the laughter, the questions (even when asked at the most inconvenient times), and the way your child runs to you for everything.

Smart: You have been given the confidence and processes that allow you to address your children's behaviors and questions—who, what, when, where, why—at age-appropriate levels and in a well-informed, peaceful way.

Pure: You know it is never too soon to develop a child's understanding about God's truth and how we all can live happy, healthy lives.

Strong, Smart, and Pure: Fast Forward ⟹ To Ages 6-10

Strong: During the "years of innocence" (ages six to puberty), you will face a wide range of challenges as children move out into school and society. Your strength of virtue is a gift to them—an example of how they need to respond when their friends and classmates expose them to outside information.

Smart: You will be shown what to continue to focus on as your children grow and develop. A close relationship with them is paramount to moving forward through these years. They will get smarter in development of faith, virtues, education, and friendships.

Pure: At this critical time in their life, make sure your children develop a deeper understanding of the need to be pure. The virtues are an "ace up your sleeve" and are guaranteed to always bring about a truthful and spiritual outlook in your children!

CHAPTER 4

LoveEd in the "Years of Innocence"

> Let the children come to me, and do
> not prevent them; for the kingdom
> of heaven belongs to such as these.
>
> —Matthew 19:14

What Exactly Are the "Years of Innocence"?

It can be said that a child is in the stage described by John Paul II as *the years of innocence* when they are about five years of age until puberty (which begins with the first signs of changes in the boy or girl's body). "This period of tranquility and serenity must never be disturbed by unnecessary information about sex. During those years, before any physical sexual development is evident, it is normal for the child's interests to turn to other aspects of life."[13]

Now that most children have mastered toilet training, managed to control tantrums, increased verbal skills, and learned to keep their hands to themselves, the child focuses more on intellectual learning. During the age of innocence, children often prefer to associate with others of their own sex, and they carefully observe the parent who is the same sex as they are, which is good for their growing sexual identity.

Education in modesty is important during this time and is usually well received. The years of innocence are a period of serenity where natural modesty can be formed; for example, they will now wear a towel when they get out of the bathtub without being told.

This stage is a time of learning to count and to read, to interact with others outside the family, and to advance in their education with certain serenity about their identity as a member of the family, as a boy or a girl, and as a child of God.

They look to their parents as role models of what it means to be a woman or a man, a mother or a father, an adult. They admire their parents and often want to be like them and help them.

The Years of Innocence Should Focus on Education, Virtues, and Growth

- Emphasize the importance of a life of personal prayer, self-control, lovingly serving others, and making good friends.

- Teach your children to speak to Jesus as a friend and guide and to be in awe of God's power as the Creator of all things.
- Self-control is one of the many virtues children can learn to practice in everyday situations of life.
- Helping around the house and being responsible for certain chores helps children begin to live for others rather than self.
- Making friends who share your family's values helps children increase their confidence in their identity as a Christian and child of God.
- Help your children to become confident in God's plan for purity of heart, mind, and soul.
    - Focus on being good, which is a constant inner battle until it becomes a habit.
    - Continue to teach the fundamentals of the faith, as well as what is morally right and wrong.
    - Teach them that purity of heart means focusing on God's will in each daily situation of life.
- Plan wholesome family activities so children learn how to have good, clean fun.
    - Laugh together, seek adventures together, and go on outings together.
    - Build family memories that bond you together in joy so children see marriage and family as a happy, safe, and secure place.

Develop Their Masculine and Feminine Strengths with Good Parenting and Role Models

During this age, girls often develop their maternal instincts through babysitting and playing with dolls, no matter how many trucks or weapons you may have in the toy box. Boys should develop a good relationship with their fathers. If Dad is missing, find another virtuous male role model to guide your son through his life—maybe an uncle or grandfather. The energetic nature of boys in this age group can lead them to more aggressive sports or nature activities that can be proper channels for their vigor. Both sexes should be encouraged to be tender and open with their families and participate in healthy physical activities. The sexual differences between male and female should neither be ignored nor minimized.

During this time, children are introduced to other role models outside of the family: teachers, coaches, parents of their friends, and so on. They will likely be drawn to others who live the values of their family. Encourage them to see the virtues in others and to practice your family virtues when they are with others. It's good for boys to identify with virtuous role models, whether it be Superman or St. Michael. It is good for girls to identify with feminine strengths, such as the persevering faith of St. Joan of Arc or the diligent practice of a successful female athlete.

Using Teachable Moments

Much of your child's ongoing education for love may take place in the short teachable moments of everyday life. You might see an inappropriate billboard while riding in the car together, an indecent photo on a magazine cover in the grocery store aisle, or an immodestly dressed person comes on the TV screen. Other teachable moments come up when your child brings home a "new word" they learned on the bus or playground or they report an experience from their friend or with a friend. These are our moments, parents, when we take a deep breath and pray for a calm reaction to our child, followed by a short, truthful response. Answers in those teachable moments should be short, truthful, and confidence building so a child knows that God and his parents know what is going on.

Indirect Answers Are Best for Sexual Questions

During this age, indirect answers are best, but always make sure the responses are rooted in truth so they can be applied later. Some basics of science and morality can accompany any questions or observations the child may have. Information should always be age-appropriate.

An example of teaching the morality without too many details would be:

> "Mommy and Daddy love each other very much. Sometimes we need some private time together."
>
> "Aunt Suzanne and Uncle Jason are having a new baby, and we are excited for them to start their family together."
>
> "We are turning off the TV after this show, since we know that the next show is bad for us to watch."

As children enter school, they often come home with questions about what they hear from others. Sometimes those questions are about sexual topics. Simple, innocent answers based in truth are best.

> "Mom, Sandy said 'sex' on the playground today. What is sex?"
>
> "Well, Kaylee, first of all, *sex* is a word that describes whether you are a boy or a girl. Sometimes you'll see it as a fill in the blank on a form to say if you're male or female, like maybe at a doctor's office. Secondly, the word *sex* is often used to describe a special holy hug that God created for moms and dads together in love. God has a great plan for moms and dads that I will tell you more about when you're older. For now, maybe you should ask Sandy to talk about some different things on the playground. What is your favorite subject to talk about?"

Sometimes adoption can bring up interesting discussions and provide teaching moments. Imagine this scenario from a child adopted from Russia as a little baby girl.

> "I'm so glad I came from Russia. I'm so glad I came from Russia!"
>
> "That's nice, Sara."
>
> "Mom, I am really, really glad I came from Russia!"
>
> "I'm glad you did, too, Sara. Why are you thinking about that today after school?"
>
> "Because Gina said she came from her mom's stomach, and that is so gross that I told her, 'I'm glad I came from Russia.'"
>
> "Oh! Now, I understand. That's cute, dear. I'm so glad you came from Russia,

too. But babies do grow inside a mother's womb, right here under her heart. And even though we adopted you from Russia, you did grow inside a woman's womb. She wasn't able to take care of you in the best way she wanted, so God sent you to us. That was His plan for our family."

Wonderful teachable moments occur when you or your child observe a woman who is pregnant. It can become an opportunity to speak of your awe for God's power to give life through us.

> "Mom, my teacher is going to have a baby. Her belly is getting real big. How does the baby get out of there?"
>
> "The baby is growing in her uterus, or womb, which is like a big hollow muscle that stretches around the baby as it grows. After nine months, the uterus muscle squeezes the baby out, and he or she is born. That is all part of God's amazing plan."

Sometimes children will act out, in a sexual way, things that they've seen on TV or at school. This may let you know that they are trying to figure out what that means. If this happens, you can say:

> "There are special hugs for the whole family and our close friends, and different special hugs for married people. God wants us to know the difference. Certain hugs and kisses are only for married people."
>
> "But I saw it on this TV show, Mom, and they were not married."
>
> "You're right, TV often shows people who are not married acting like they *are* married. God must be sad when He sees that. I'm sad about that, too, so I turn the TV off right away when I see people offending God. God has a special plan for marriage that He doesn't want people to waste outside of marriage."

Explain this in a way that helps them begin to see the difference between healthy passion (in marriage) and brotherly affection (that we can display in a non-sexual way with our friends and relatives).

During the age of innocence, a parent at home can present the wonder and awe of fetal development in gentle and sacred language, especially if a new baby is coming into the family. New information can gradually build on what they already know.

For example, when you pray the Hail Mary, or after saying the Rosary, you can ask your child:

> "Do you know what a 'womb' is when we say, 'Blessed is the fruit of your womb'?
> God made the womb to be a safe place for a baby to grow for nine months before it is born. The womb is also called the uterus."

Using a simple pro-life book that shows fetal development can be a good way to teach the wonder, awe, and fascination of the growth of a child in the womb.

Another innocent way to teach respect for life at this age is to read the Dr. Seuss book *Horton Hears a Who*, which teaches that "a person is a person, no matter how small."

Innocent, Not Ignorant—A True Story from Coleen on a Teachable Moment

When my seven-year-old sister and I were having a private conversation with my mom, my sister asked my mom, "What's a honeymoon for?" My mother responded, "A honeymoon is the first vacation that a man and a woman can take together after they're married, since now they are a new family. A honeymoon is the time when they learn how to get dressed and undressed in the same bedroom together. Before their wedding, that would not be right to do, so now they can practice being more comfortable together as they start their new family. Now that they are married, they can sleep together, too. So a honeymoon celebrates their marriage; it should be a fun first vacation for the couple that helps bond them as a new family for God."

It wasn't until years later when I was on a date that I realized how much my mother taught me in that explanation. My date was playing with the top buttons of my blouse and the Holy Spirit brought to my mind my mom's story. I thought to myself, *This is not a honeymoon, so I better get his hands off my clothes*. And I let him know I was off-limits.

My mother had answered my sister's question with the truth that a seven-year-old should know, filled it with God's plan, and left the direct information between the lines.

As I matured, those innocent lessons became clearer. Between the lines, I learned:

- Keep your clothes on until after marriage.
- Don't sleep together until your honeymoon.
- God has a time and plan for newlyweds to get used to being together.
- Living together or getting undressed outside of marriage is not good or needed.

Correct Any Erroneous Information

If you suspect that your child is picking up sexual information from others or from the media, it doesn't hurt to open up the subject for them when you have some private time together. Casually bring up topics of love and life during teachable moments in the news or in your extended family. Correct any erroneous information your children may pick up from others, keeping explanations simple and always giving the moral explanation: "This is how God made it to be, and I bet you want to live God's way, don't you?"

Another example of a teachable moment is a child who watched a commercial about erectile dysfunction on television and later saw a large advertisement billboard about ED on the highway. He said to his dad in the car:

> "Dad, Jared said that ED means (**bleep**). Is that true?"

Trying not to appear shocked, his dad responded:

> "Not exactly, son. Let me help you understand what that means. That billboard and the commercials are for a medicine that helps men's bodies if something in their private area doesn't work properly. The E stands for erectile, and the D stands for dysfunction. Dysfunction means that something doesn't work, and you already know that an erection is when you are excited or bored and your penis gets stiff. I will teach you more about this when you are older since it is something you do not need to know too much about while you are a kid, okay?"

Usually a child in this age of innocence will file this information away in the "later" box in their mind.

Your child comes home from school and asks:

"What does (**bleep**) mean?"

You can tell that they instinctively know it's a bad word.

"Where did you learn that word, Tommy?"

"Max said it on the playground today."

"That is a nasty word that people should not say."

"What does it mean, Mom?"

"It means that someone is doing something wrong with his or her body. It is a disrespectful word that we don't want to listen to or use. Let's always use words that respect ourselves and others, okay?"

Teachable Moments for More Delicate Issues

Abortion

Your ten-year-old sees some literature that says, "Stop Abortion." She asks you, "What is abortion?"

"Abortion is very sad. It is killing a baby while it is still growing in its mother's womb."

"Why would someone do that, Mom?"

"It's hard to understand that, Janie. Maybe the woman was confused or scared, or she didn't realize what she was doing."

"Isn't that like murder?"

"Yes, it is, but for some strange reason, people still have abortions legally. We as Catholics know that is wrong, so we do everything we can to stop people from having abortions and to help mothers so they do not even want to have an abortion. Many good people are even trying to change the laws that legalize abortion. God loves all babies, and He wants all moms to love their babies, too. Let us pray that all abortion will stop. Hail Mary . . ."

Rape

How to answer a question about rape for a more innocent child can be very difficult. For example, if your nine-year-old daughter hears about rape on the news, you can explain it this way:

"That was a very sad story, wasn't it, Kaitlin? Do you understand what rape means?"

"Well, sort of."

"You know that not everyone in the world is good. And some people can even take something good and use it for something bad. Going to the bank is good, but robbing a bank is not. Driving a car can be good, but driving so fast that you kill or hurt others in an accident is not good."

"I know that part, Mom, but what is rape?"

"God gave us free will so we can choose to do good or evil. Rape is a crime; it is an evil way of a man forcing himself upon a woman to use her body in a way that God did not intend. The rapist turns an act that was supposed to be good for husbands and wives into a way to hurt a person."

"What did he do, Mom?"

"He took her clothes off and forced a private part of his body on her."

"Yuck, why would someone do that?"

"There are some mentally sick people in the world who commit such crimes. Remember the story of Maria Goretti? Her family's farmworker tried to force her to do something impure with him, and she refused. She said she would rather die than sin."

"I didn't know this news story was like the Maria Goretti story."

"You will probably not be asked to be a martyr for purity like Maria Goretti, but you do need to know that rape is a serious crime. Let's say a prayer for that poor girl in the news who was the victim of rape, and the sick rapist who is the criminal, that he will be converted."

"What should I do if someone ever tries to do that to me?"

"Scream for help and run away if you can."

"Okay, Mom. I think I will always stay close to you."

Pornography

Another example might be an eight-year-old child who came across some pornography when a computer movie ended.

"Mom, I saw someone on the computer without any clothes on."

"What did you do?"

"I saw it was a private part like yours, and I looked at it, and then I turned it off."

"I'm so sorry that someone put that on the Internet for you to see. That person was wrong. It wasn't your fault. You were right to turn it off. Did seeing that make you want to look at it again?"

"No, not really."

"That's good that you turned it off right away, because sometimes naked images of people or even cartoons can make you want to look more. But those are bad pictures put up there by people who do not respect the human body. Our private parts are good, but they should always be kept private."

"Oh, I didn't know that could happen, but I thought it was weird when I saw it on my computer."

"I am going to check to see if we can get another filter to block out that bad stuff, but if you see it again, turn off the computer right away, look away, and say a prayer."

"Okay, Mom."

Homosexuality

The question of homosexuality can hardly be avoided today, even for small children. A simple answer for younger children can avoid judgment yet still teach a simple scientific truth to build on later such as:

"Dad, is it okay to have two dads, instead of one dad and one mom?"

"That's not how God created us, son."

"But Jake has two dads and no mom."

"Well, that might seem to be the case, but every human person has one mother and one father somewhere. God has created us that way since Adam and Eve. Maybe Jake's mom couldn't help his dad take care of him, so his real dad found a friend to help him."

"Oh. Well, how about you and Mom—will you always stay together to take care of me?"

"Yes, we will, by the grace of God. Let's say a prayer now for all children and marriages. Hail Mary . . ."

Teaching the Sixth and Ninth Commandments in the Years of Innocence

When you're teaching your children the Ten Commandments (as six- to eight-year-olds should learn), help them examine their consciences and prepare them for their first confession. This can include explanations of all the commandments. Read the *Catechism* on the moral life if you need to study up first. After you talk about honoring God and one's parents, you will cover killing and hurting people, lying and stealing, etc.

When you teach the sixth and ninth commandments, use general language. You can explain them to your child this way:

"The sixth commandment is 'Thou shalt not commit adultery.' There are certain hugs and kisses that God only intended for married couples, and they are wrong to do if you are not married. Adultery is a sin against the faithfulness of marriage. Adultery means that someone went out on a date or hugged and kissed in a married way with someone he or she is not married to. That's why this is sometimes called 'cheating.' It's stealing the affection that only belongs to the married couple. God wants all people to be faithful to marriage, and your faithfulness to God begins now, even before you have met the person you are going to marry."

"The ninth commandment is 'You shall not covet your neighbor's wife.' It instructs us to not look at people as just bodies, to not think about touching their private parts or want to use them as objects. We should not 'want' to use our own or anyone else's bodies as playthings."

"Sometimes even the magazines in the grocery store do that by showing pictures of people hardly wearing any clothes. The publishers want people to buy those magazines, so they try to make us curious. We call this 'indecency' since God made our private parts to be private, and he wants us to see each other for our goodness and virtue, not just as our bodies."

"God wants us to be respectful of all people and look at them as His beloved creatures. Besides magazines, sometimes the TV or computer may show people immodestly dressed or without any clothes. If you ever see indecency like that, look away immediately and say a prayer to avoid sinning against the ninth commandment. If you saw it already and didn't know it was wrong, it was not a sin, but you can still take it to Jesus for healing."

Media Awareness for Parents with Young Children

Keep a careful, prudent, and watchful use of the media your children may be exposed to in order to avoid polluting their minds or making sin seem normal. Monitor your television viewing. Screen the music or radio stations you listen to. This information does not just "go over their heads," as some people may think. The information your children view goes right into their subconscious minds, whether or not you think they are aware of it.

Apologize to your children if something comes over the airwaves that may be offensive to their innocence, and then say a prayer for purity, such as the Hail Mary. Teach your children to stand up for goodness when they are at a friend's house and someone wants to watch a show that is harmful, evil, or indecent. As you well know, evil is all around us, and the growing digital world gives us access to a wide variety of good and evil.

Guidance from the Church

To resolve the problem of a child receiving information from mass media or their peers who have received premature sexual information, parents can begin to give carefully limited sexual information to correct immoral and erroneous information or to control obscene language.

During the years of innocence, children should also be protected as much as possible from "adult" sexual themes and entertainment.

Premature sexual information should never be imposed on children for educational intent. It is difficult enough to help them prepare to face the unplanned exposure. Yet, people may ask, why not give children all the information at an early age? The Pontifical Council for the Family reminds us why.

"At this stage of development, children are still not capable of fully understanding the value of the affective dimension of sexuality" because they are not psychologically able to "integrate premature sexual information with moral responsibility. Such information tends to shatter their emotional and educational development and to disturb the natural serenity of this period of life."[14] Thus, premature sexual information is counterproductive to proper education if the child's mind cannot process the information properly.

This is an important reason parents should be careful to teach their children only simple truths during this stage. That's why *LoveEd* has two different levels of information—one for puberty and one for the young adolescent.

Pornography on the Prowl

Today, we unfortunately need to "porn-proof" our kids by teaching them how to avoid and reject pornography if they are accidentally exposed to it and to flee from it if they have been exposed to it regularly. Explain that pornography includes inappropriate pictures or movies of people either without clothes or dressed scantily. Let your children know it is wrong for people to take those pictures or for anyone to look at them. You can say:

> "It's not only wrong to look at pornography, it's also sad that some people let themselves be used for pictures like that. Pornography is wrong, but some people make money using people this way and getting other people to look at them. They must not know how much God loves them, or they would not misuse their bodies like that. Remember this Psalm whenever you hear or see something pornographic: 'A clean heart create for me, God; renew within me a steadfast spirit' (Ps 51:12)."

Safety from Predators

Repeat the safety information to avoid predators that you taught your children when they were toddlers:

> "Never let anyone see or touch or take pictures of your private parts. If someone asks you to do that, tell him or her *no* really loudly, run away, and find a grown-up to help you. Come tell us right away. It is wrong, even if you know the person and he or she says it is okay. There is a sickness of the mind that makes some people want to do bad things. I am sorry that you have to know about these things, but we want you to be safe."

In addition to these simple safety warnings, you can teach your child the difference in boundaries between a good affectionate touch and something that is unacceptable. Explain that they should avoid or report any inappropriate touches from other children, teens, and adults, even people they know. Remind them of this lesson as they go out and participate in activities outside of the family, whether it is for sports teams, school trips, or children's camps. Warn them that someone they even already know might try to touch them inappropriately, and always to resist bad touches and tell a trusted adult about it.

To learn other ways to prevent child sexual abuse for your child and others, at school or in your extended family, or to create safety plans for times that your child is away from home, learn more at stopitnow.org. The site can also help you learn the warning signs of sexual abuse.

Real Questions from Real Parents

For almost twenty years, I have been hosting a live call-in radio show on Catholic Radio. Among the variety of problems I address for the callers, concerned parents often call in with questions regarding their child's education in sexuality. Here are a few common questions I have received over the years, along with my responses.

How to correct misinformation when a child learns about sexual information from friends

Dear Coleen,

My eight-year-old daughter came home and told me a neighbor girl said that sex is when a boy puts his penis into a girl's vagina. She wants to know if this is true, and she is also asking how someone can get pregnant when she's not married. My three other younger children were present, and I told my daughter that she and I would discuss this later alone. Do you have any advice on how to approach this with her? I could give her a brief explanation and say that it's just like anything else where God lets us go against his plan if we choose to. Also, I'm inclined to keep her away from these neighbor kids because of this and other reasons. My husband feels that this is sheltering her too much because we homeschool her. We do participate in a lot of homeschooling activities with other children at least four days a week, however.

Thank you for your advice,

Lois

Dear Lois,

You have the right idea. Give a simple explanation, but in the context of what the other kids don't yet know. Tell her that her friend was partially right. Your conversation might go something like this:

> "God does have a plan for a husband and wife to come so close together in a holy embrace that the 'two become one flesh,' as the Bible says. In this holy embrace of marriage, the husband and wife can join their private parts together. The husband can plant the seed of life to join with his wife's egg cell, and she can get pregnant that way. God's law teaches that we should only get that close to someone when we are married. But someone who is not married, and who doesn't listen to God, might act that way and pretend it doesn't matter if they are married or not. That's how a woman gets pregnant outside of marriage. This greatly saddens God because He wants all children to be born into a loving marriage. We live in a crazy world where people ignore God. But how about you? Do you want to follow God throughout your life?"
>
> "Yes, Mom, I do."
>
> "I thought you did, and you know that I will always help you do that."

Tell your daughter that in your family, you plan to follow God in all things, and one of those is to only do married things after you are married; that's what the sixth commandment teaches us. If we ever mess up and disobey God, even in little ways, we can say we are sorry and seek His forgiveness in confession. Also, tell her that it is not right to discuss these kinds of topics outside of the family. Remind her that her friends don't always have the right information but that she can always come to you with any questions she might have.

God bless you,

Coleen

What to do about a child who discovers pornography

Dear Coleen,

I recently realized that my nine-year-old daughter has been "googling" sexual terminology. It goes without saying that she can no longer be on the computer without me or my husband in the room with her. I have told her that what she did was wrong, and I've asked her to tell me if she has any questions. I don't know what else I should say or do. I know kids get curious about body parts, etc., at this age, but I really thought she was *way* too young for me to be concerned about her searching the Internet for this. We are in shock and need guidance.

Thank you,

Suzanne

Dear Suzanne,

It sounds as though your daughter is bright and curious. You did the right thing by taking her off the computer. It would also be good to satisfy her curiosity in other, more appropriate ways. First, I would suggest teaching her about her other bodily systems—her digestive system, nervous system, and so on—using children's science books from the library or bookstore. Look for some with great diagrams or transparencies so she can see the organs from the inside. There are also some good videos available on the Internet, but stay away from those depicting the reproductive system where you may get some inappropriate sidebars. Let your daughter get to know her other body systems first and be fascinated with them. This should satisfy her curiosity for now, and you can let her know that there is a special system that will develop when she is a teenager called the reproductive system and you will teach her more about that when she gets a little older.

You can teach her now what will happen to her body in menstruation and explain how a baby grows inside a mother's womb if you think she is ready for that information. Listen for questions if she brings up the sexual act, and refer to it as the marriage act. Give her simple, innocent, general explanations, avoiding a discussion of intercourse for now. You can speak instead of a holy embrace and the sacredness of her body. Teach her about the saints as role models for virtue so she can be fascinated with their lives. It is not necessary that all her curiosities be answered, but you want to make sure her questions are addressed in light of God's plan for us.

As you teach her about how her body works, let her know there are certain subjects we should not look up on the Internet or talk about with friends, because they are private. Let her know that many people teach about sexual topics wrongly or disrespectfully. We want to learn about our bodies in a beautiful way, which is God's way. Tell her that if she sees some immodest or sexual pictures on the Internet, she should turn off the computer immediately and say a prayer so she doesn't remember any of the wrong ideas that can harm her.

When you are confident that she can discipline herself, you can cautiously allow her to return to a supervised use of computers.

God bless you,

Coleen

What to do about my eight-year-old son's exposure to indecency

Dear Coleen,

I went to a restaurant with my wife and two sons, ages seven and eight. While waiting for our food, on one of the many televisions facing my older son and my wife, a music video came on showing an extremely vulgar rap artist simulating sex with a woman. When my little boy saw this, he looked very disgusted. I'm not sure what to say to him to follow up. My wife and I have never discussed the perversions of the world with either of my two sons. We do discuss the importance of modesty and decency. Do you have advice for us in this situation?

My most sincere thanks to any thought on this matter,

George

Dear George,

Since your son is above the age of reason, you can explain how this video showed both the good and evil in the world. You can respond to his look of disgust by saying:

> "I saw that look of disgust on your face when you saw that dirty dancer show up on the TV screen in the restaurant. I'm glad that you were disgusted. That's how a Christian responds when someone is doing something so offensive. They were

doing something wrong with their bodies, and you knew that was wrong, so good for you. I am sorry you had to see such a sin. Sin is all around us, but as much as we can, we want to avoid seeing it and doing it.

"God made our bodies to do good—to glorify Him. But a lot of people do not obey God. They often don't realize that they should not use their bodies disrespectfully. They mock the beauty that God gave us by their immodesty and dirty dancing. People sometimes even say vulgar words that are also sinful. This hurts our dignity as children of God.

"Son, you are pure and have a good conscience. Christians should always act and dress in ways that glorify God, no matter how old we are.

"Let's pray that you will always obey and glorify God with your body and do good and kind things."

God bless you for being a good dad,

Coleen

Activities for Parents to Reinforce Virtue Concepts With Their Children

A good song to sing with your young child is "Oh, Be Careful Little Eyes What You See" (sung to the tune of "If You're Happy and You Know It"). It's fun to sing now as a child, and the lesson will stay with your child into adolescence, and maybe into adulthood.

> Oh, be careful little eyes what you see
> Oh, be careful little eyes what you see
> 'Cause the Father up above is looking down in love
> Oh, be careful little eyes what you see.

Other verses to sing include:

> Be careful little ears what you hear . . .
> Oh be careful little Tom what you say . . .
> Oh be careful little feet where you go . . .

Another good virtue song would be to sing the "Patience Song" (to the tune of "Twinkle, Twinkle, Little Star").

> I am patient, I can wait
> When you're busy when you're late.
> I won't cry and I won't whine,
> I'll wait for my turn and time.
> I am patient, I can wait when you're busy, when you're late.

Strong, Smart, and Pure: During the Years of Innocence ⟹ Rewind

Strong: While your children are young, you will face a wide range of opportunities to help them be innocent, but not ignorant. You are your children's strongest advocate in helping them live the virtues and keeping their minds and hearts pure.

Smart: Teach your children simple moral truths now so that they will be smart about purity. Give them the confidence to come to you for answers so they will be smart about their bodies and souls, smart about being safe, and smart about family values.

Pure: This is a critical time to make sure your children are developing a deeper understanding of the need to be pure. Help them protect their innocence by keeping a careful watch on the media they use.

Strong, Smart, and Pure: Fast Forward ⟹ To Puberty

Strong: As your children approach puberty, their strength in virtue should grow. They should be choosing virtue, even when you are not looking. Virtue is more than obedience; as they get older, virtue means knowing how to act on their own, too.

Smart: You will learn what to continue to focus on as your children grow and develop. Besides having a close relationship with them by engaging in activities and conversations, you will find time to teach them the sacred science behind their changing bodies. As the topics get bigger, help them concentrate on continuing to develop their faith, virtues, education, hobbies/activities, and relationships with others.

Pure: Puberty adds another level of love education. Purity now comes to mean more as romantic desires rise. The virtue of chastity is required so your children can maintain their purity and become truly loving persons.

CHAPTER 5

LoveEd for Puberty

Human life is a gift received in order then to be given as a gift.
—Pope St. John Paul II

The third stage for sexual education is just before puberty, sometime between the ages of ten and fourteen. The timing for teaching new information will be different for girls than for boys, and it will often depend on the child's level of innocence or curiosity. Education in virtue must continue to be strengthened as the child grows more independent. Learning to get along in friendship groups outside the family will help them with social development and moral decision making. But stronger internal virtues will be needed to resist peer pressure. Help your children develop the courage to do the right thing, even when you are not there to supervise and their friends want to do something wrong.

Education about the changes to take place during puberty should be presented in a positive and practical setting over time, but reviewed in more detail when puberty is imminent. A child should have time to process the information and know the general moral principles of chastity before they are given information about the conjugal union, fertilization, and conception.

Help Your Children Prepare for Upcoming Changes

Additional education about the growing body is required for children approaching puberty. It's good for children to be confident and well prepared for the emotional, mental, and physical changes about to take place. Their greatest confidence in life will come from the fact that God loves each person intimately and individually with a love that is indescribable. God's love is faithful and freely given and will be present with them each day of their lives, especially in difficult times. This knowledge and awareness can help preteens know they are never alone and always loved.

LoveEd Teaches That Love Is Sacrifice

In order for children to learn how to live a life of love, they need to practice making sacrifices throughout their lives. They will not automatically become "other-centered" instead of "self-centered" the day they get married. God's grace works with our nature, so a child's nature, as we mentioned in the young child section, needs to be predisposed to chastity by learning to make sacrifices and wait. Emphasize the importance of sacrifice in your family, not just during Lent, but all year. Challenge your children to make sacrifices cheerfully rather than complain and criticize. These are good habits to develop whether they are called to marriage, religious life, or the single life.

During puberty, children become physically stronger in between the awkwardness of growth spurts. They can take on greater physical challenges besides the spiritual ones; some examples include lifting heavy loads, carrying in the groceries, taking out the garbage, and putting the laundry away. Help your children learn that sacrifices, by becoming a habit now, will make them more loving when they are adults.

Help Them Improve Their Decision-Making Skills

The age of puberty is also a good time for teaching some critical analysis skills for making intelligent judgments about what they see, hear, and read. They need an objective measuring stick– God's truth–in order to make those daily assessments when they face temptations to cheat, be rude or mouthy, shoplift, or engage in bad attitudes and wrong actions. Teach them how to think through issues.

Their social life and school culture will also need to be assessed and critiqued to help them identify and understand the true meaning of beauty, marriage, honesty, faithfulness, and their own bodies.

Give Them Examples to Manage Their Emotions

Puberty is a time to learn to better manage changing emotions, such as irritability, anger, sadness, impatience, frustration, insecurity, and jealousy so children do not punish everyone around them with whatever they might be feeling at the moment. Their feelings can fool them into making bad decisions, such as breaking something, eating excess food for comfort, or shouting at and hurting someone with their words or actions. Emotions are to be acknowledged and examined so children can get to know themselves better. Often children will feel bad about themselves after losing their temper and lashing out. This is a normal and healthy reaction, and it also provides a time to help them think through how to manage their behavior when they're feeling irritable. Discuss with your children how to be calm when they feel moody. Help them learn how to communicate with words–whether in writing or peaceful conversations–after they have cooled off and gathered their thoughts.

Unfortunately, the feeling of invincibility in a prideful child during puberty may lead a preteen to think, *That's just how I am, so deal with it.* This is harmful to the family, to all relationships, and to the child's social maturity. It's important for preteens to learn *now* how to be kind to others, even when they're feeling bad about themselves. Discuss with them some constructive things they can do when they *feel* out of control so they don't *act* out of control. Sometimes deeper needs must be addressed, or perhaps more love and attention (or more structure and discipline) are required. Sometimes children just need to burn excess energy with healthy physical activity. Human beings should feel, think, and then act according to their God-given dignity.

Feelings of attraction for the opposite sex may arise at this age, too. These feelings could lead to good friendships or bad relationships, depending on whether children are using their brains to make their decisions or just using their emotions. As they get older, children need to be warned that feelings of attraction could lead them to try to get the attention of someone in the wrong way, or could lead them into a harmful relationship. Unlike what they may see in the media or at school, all feelings of attraction do not need to be acted upon. It's better to be a friend than a flirt. It's better to work together on a service project than to begin adult social activities during the elementary and middle school years. Keeping boy-girl activities away from the pairing-off realm will lead to better relationships in the long run.

Strengthen the Parent/Child Bond

It's also good for children to solidify strong relationships with each parent during this time in order to insure healthy sexual development. Quite often, up until this age, a majority of children have a mother as their primary caregiver, so they already know how to interact well with her. But at this age, a father's role is also increasingly important.

A girl's relationship with her father is crucial to the development of her sexual identity as a woman. Her relationship with him will also affect the choices she makes about which kind of boys to like. Dad can take her out on "dates" and teach her how she should be treated by men. If she does not have a good relationship with her dad, an effort should be made to help her develop a relationship with a trusted uncle or grandfather. Otherwise, without such a relationship in her life, she may seek to fulfill those needs with the boys she is attracted to and sour a potential relationship due to her neediness.

A father's relationship with his son is also crucial to a boy's sexual development as a man. A boy looks to his father as an example of how to treat women with respect. He watches carefully how his dad treats his mother, and he often wants to be like him. It's also a good idea for a mom to spend time with her son alone once in a while and talk about how to treat women with respect.

In today's sexually confused world, children are even wondering what it means to be a boy or a girl; many of them are struggling to identify with their biological sex. You can help them understand that there is a science behind our male or female gender. Each person is born as either a male or a female baby. The male baby grows to become a boy who eventually develops into a man. The female baby grows to become a girl who blossoms into a woman. The image and dignity of God is given to both wonderfully created sexes. It's good to appreciate our gender—male or female—and live out God's plan for us. If a child has a serious problem with his or her sexual identity, parents should seek professional help from a therapist who implements the Catholic faith into the practice (see NARTH.com).

Encourage Healthy Friendships

Both boys and girls between the ages of ten to fourteen should learn to develop good friendships with members of both their own sex and the opposite sex. Good friendships with the same gender will help them grow in trust and confidence and give them a support system for living virtue. Virtuous friendships during these years can help your child grow in selflessness, confidence, and courage. Get to know your children's friends and their friends' parents. Help your child think about the qualities of a good friend—what it means to both be a good friend and find a good friend.

In addition to the virtues they learn within the family, the friendship circle requires some additional virtues, since friendship has to be earned. Some virtues children can practice in these friendships are cooperation, compromise (on non-moral issues), leadership, fair play, joy in wholesome fun, trust, kindness, and honesty. Friendship means supporting one another to be good and do good, and it involves being there for them whether they're having a good day or a bad day.

Boy-girl friendships at this age are best kept to a sibling-like affection rather than acting out attempts at romantic love. This is true for quite a few more years while your child matures emotionally, is strengthened morally, and has the fortitude to always do the right thing when peer pressure is strong. It's important to realize that friendship does not include pairing off, flirting, or trying to get the attention of the opposite sex.

They should look for friends who want to be good and develop virtuous habits. Through curfews and family rules, you can slow down pairing off too soon and romantic emotional attachments during this time.

Parents should teach their children that men and women are different, yet complementary—and created to work together for the good of society. Boys should treat girls with additional courtesy and respect during puberty, and they should always be expected to show good manners. As your child matures, it is important to tell them that men's minds are wired differently than women's. Boys see and react differently than girls do. This is true of their emotions, their thoughts, and their physical reactions and activities. Discuss the differences between what boys like and what girls like and how they react differently to different circumstances.

Show Them Real Inner Beauty

God sees each of us as beautiful. It's important that we also see God's beauty in each individual. He made each of us unique, according to the genetic makeup of our parents. How boring it would be if everyone looked the same! So why try to make yourself look like someone else? Why compare yourself to others?

We should teach our children to thank God for the beautiful body he gave them—now, and as it changes.

To help your children see that the lasting nature of inner beauty is different (and far more valuable) than the culture's fleeting view of superficial beauty, ask your son or daughter these questions:

- How would you define beauty? Do you think your grandmother is beautiful? Why?
- What are three things that make a woman beautiful?
- What does TV tell you about what makes a woman beautiful?
- What makes a man handsome?
- Does TV see beauty the way that God does?

Show your children examples of God's beauty—both in nature and in the virtues you see in them and their friends. Affirm the goodness and beauty you see in the world so they can identify it and look for it. Take time to see a great sunset or look at the night sky. Notice the beauty you see in their souls as they show concern for others, help around the house without asking, patiently babysit for the neighbors, or care for younger siblings.

Help Your Children Mature in Their Prayer Life

Regular daily prayer during puberty and adolescence is important; teach your children how much God loves them and wants to hear from them frequently throughout the day. Their personal relationship with God should be nurtured so that they know He is the best friend and guide they will ever have. Show them what God's love looks like by your kindness, patience, and mercy. Introduce them to role models of purity, such as Mary and Joseph and the virgin saints.

A deeper prayer life is important during this time, when children going through puberty sometimes feel alone or misunderstood. They should know that they have friends in Jesus, Mary, and all the saints, whether or not they have a good friend on earth. Teach them how to talk to God from their hearts besides praying the common prayers of the Church and meditating on the mysteries of the Rosary.

How can we teach this? First of all, by praying as a family. But then, as your children mature, take some time to pray with them privately so they learn to have more personal conversations with God. Bring them to Mass or to adoration for some quiet time in front of Jesus, who is present in the tabernacle. Teach them how to read and pray with Scripture verses, starting with the Psalms, Proverbs, and Gospels. They can read a few verses at a time and then stop and listen to what God might be saying to them in that passage. Memorizing a psalm or proverb a week will keep God's Word in their minds and hearts.

Guide Them to Strengthen Their Character

Character traits, virtues, and the will to choose the good should be strengthened during these years so children are prepared to resist the temptations that come during the teen years. Help them understand that they have a part of their soul that chooses, called free will, and a thinking part of their soul, called intellect. They also need to know that while their emotions or feelings may affect them, feelings are often not a good basis for decision-making. Instead, they need to follow their well-formed conscience, which is that voice of God that speaks to the heart. Their conscience should be informed by the Ten Commandments, the teachings of the Church, the Beatitudes, and the words of Jesus in the Gospels.

A child's character is strengthened when he or she makes decisions based on what we should do from a moral standpoint, not what we feel like doing. Growing in virtues such as diligence, perseverance, and faithfulness will help children get strong on the inside and help them make good decisions. Examples might be sticking with their music lesson, working toward that final belt level in martial arts, or challenging themselves to increase their strength and speed for the track team.

Faithfulness can be practiced by being loyal and sticking up for family members, being honest when everyone else is cheating, or promising to do homework without being told.

The virtue of chastity should be introduced as a special gift from God to practice purity, help discover their vocation, and prepare them for a total self-gift to God or to their future spouse if marriage is in their future. At this stage of puberty, as they learn more about their growing bodies, it is very important to learn and practice purity of mind, words, thoughts, and deeds.

Review Safety and Boundaries

Review with your children the child safety and protection information you taught them when they were younger. Add the fact that there are some people who have sick minds and abuse people by asking them to look at indecent pictures, showing them private body parts, or touching them in private places. Remind them to *never* undress for anyone or let any person touch them in a private body place. This is wrong, and remind them to say *no*, run away from the situation, and come tell you or a trusted adult. This is what they should do even if they know the person and he or she told them not to tell anyone. Tell anyway!

As your child is developing sexually during puberty, it is also helpful to warn them that sometimes a person they know, or even a boyfriend or girlfriend they like, may attempt to touch them in a sexual way. This is also wrong and a form of sexual harassment or sexual abuse. Some teens or preteens might start this at a game or as a dare, but it is still wrong and should be avoided. If this happens to them, let your child know they should call home right away and you will come pick them up. Inappropriate touching should never be a game. It is always disrespectful.

Alcohol, Safety, and Bad Decisions

You can also warn your children that another way kids can be persuaded to do something wrong is by giving them alcohol. Instruct them never to drink alcohol at this age. Alcohol shuts down the ability of the brain to make a good decision. Under the influence of alcohol, people often resort to doing whatever they feel like doing at the moment, even if they know it's wrong. Many young people and adults make regrettable and dangerous decisions they might not have made had they not been under the influence of alcohol.

Prepare Them for Puberty

Before puberty approaches, children should be aware of the changes that are to take place as their bodies begin to mature. The reproductive system does not fully function in their bodies until puberty, although most other systems function fully from birth. God has programmed puberty to begin between the ages of eleven and fifteen, but it could happen sooner or later and still be considered normal.

Some signs of puberty beginning might be:

- Increased perspiration or body odor
- Unexpected emotional changes
- Growth spurt and weight gain
- Additional hair growth in underarms and near genitals
- Increased oiliness in hair or on the face
- Girls: breast buds develop, hips widen, menstruation begins
- Boys: voice deepens, hair in beard area darkens, testosterone increases aggressive energy

Personal Hygiene

It will continue to be the parent's responsibility to train their children in personal hygiene, even though the health textbooks in school often cover this. Puberty adds a new dimension to the need for personal hygiene: your child will experience an increase in perspiration, girls will need to know about sanitary supplies, and boys might need to be encouraged to wash their hair more often if it becomes oily. The best approach is to speak of hygiene as a way of growing up and deciding on their own to be clean and neat, not just to follow their parents' orders. And remember, when the hormones of sexual attraction begin, your children might just want to look neat and clean to impress others. Then you may have the opposite problem of *too* much bathroom time!

Breast Development: God's Plan for Mothers and Babies

The information you give to your children about breast development will vary from boys to girls.

Breast Development Information for Girls

Let's imagine how a conversation might go between a mother and her daughter:

"Sarah, do you remember last year when Aunt Jenny had a baby and she nursed her?"

"Uh-huh."

"Did you ever stop to think what an amazing system God placed in women's bodies to help us feed a baby after it's born?"

"I guess not."

"In the culture we live in today, many women seem more concerned about their bra size and how much breast they show than about God's amazing plan."

"Yeah, Katie's mom got her a bra last week. Do you think I can get one, too?"

"Getting your first bra is one of those exciting times of life, isn't it? It's one way to feel more grown up. Do you know what a bra is for, Sarah?"

"I guess so."

"A bra is both for modesty and support."

"I don't have anything to support yet."

"That's okay. We could get you a sports bra for the modesty part. God is preparing you to be a mother someday, whether or not you will ever become one! God made women's bodies this way. Tiny glands called mammary glands will soon begin to grow inside your breasts. Your breasts already have muscle tissue and fatty tissue over your ribs, and the milk ducts will grow between those. Besides the milk glands that make the milk, small ducts will grow connecting the glands to the outside of the body to hold the milk until the baby suckles it."

"How long does the milk stay in there, Mom?"

"Oh, I forgot to mention this, Sarah: While your mammary glands and milk ducts will start developing now, they do not finish developing unless you get pregnant. It's during that time that your body starts preparing to make milk."

"Oh, good."

"Then, after the baby is born, the mom's hormones signal the mammary glands to start making milk."

"How does the mom's body know how much milk to make?"

"It adjusts to make as much milk as the baby needs each day. It's another one of God's amazing plans. So for now, when your breasts start developing, you may feel a small bump behind the nipple. It may even itch or be tender. That's why we will get you a bra for support and protection. Modesty is another whole issue. As you start developing breasts, your nipples will get bigger, and you need to wear a bra so they don't show through your shirt."

"Wow, Mom, thanks! I wanted to get a bra now that Katie did, but I'm also glad I don't have to worry about making milk for a long time."

"We will talk about modesty more when we go shopping. As you start changing from a girl to a woman, you will need to be extra careful to dress with dignity so people don't just look at you as a body. You want them to notice your face and beautiful personality first."

Breast Development Information for Boys

Now, let's imagine how a conversation might go between a father and his son:

"Son, do you remember when your mom breastfed your little sister, Anna?"

"Well, kind of. I was only five, so I wasn't paying that much attention."

"It's good for mothers to nurse their babies like Mom did for you and Anna. Not everyone appreciates their bodies or uses them as God intends. Sometimes people use their bodies to show off or get attention. I noticed that those cheerleaders on TV were missing some parts of their shirts—did you see that? They sure didn't get their money's worth."

"Duh, Dad."

"Did you know it's not right for women to show off their bodies like that?"

"They looked fine to me, Dad; don't make a big deal about it."

"Son, do you know why God made women's breasts? It wasn't to show them bouncing at a football game or a dance. God made women's breasts with milk ducts in them to feed their babies."

"So does that mean these cheerleaders have a lot of milk?"

"Not necessarily, son. Women's breasts come in all shapes and sizes, but they're all designed to produce milk for a baby. The milk isn't made until after a baby is born, though. It's actually wrong for guys to look at women's bodies as objects. We should see girls as someone's future wife or mother. It's too bad that the cheerleaders show off like that because it naturally makes us want to look more, doesn't it?"

"Yeah, sometimes it does, Dad."

"What do you think we should think about when we look away?"

"Obviously not that girl's body; maybe scoring a hockey goal, or climbing that mountain at the park without running out of breath."

"Good idea, son. When you see a woman, it would also be good to see her as mom someday, just as you saw your mom nursing your little sister when she was a baby. That is why God gave women breasts—for breastfeeding their babies."

Menstruation Education for Girls

Girls need more information about menstruation than boys do at this age (although boys do need to know some things). You should explain clearly to your daughter what she should expect, whether or not you think she has picked up the information along the way. Reviewing this together can help form the bond between you to discuss other more intimate topics. Don't miss an opportunity to spend time alone with her.

You might have a conversation with your daughter that goes like this:

"Before we find out about menstruation, which is another word for having your period, first let's review the organs inside a woman's body. God created girls with two ovaries and one uterus, both hidden safely inside her abdomen. The ovaries are almond-shaped organs on each side of the uterus. The Fallopian tubes connect the ovaries to the uterus. The uterus is also called the womb; it's a hollow, pear-shaped organ that opens up into the vagina. The vagina leads to the outside of the body. Only girls have this tiny opening, and it is safely hidden between the opening for urination and the rectal opening for bowel movements. The vagina is also called the birth canal, and it stretches open around the baby's head when it's time for the baby to be delivered."

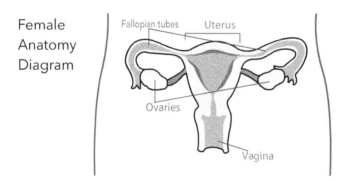

Female Anatomy Diagram

Show your daughter the pictures and point out those parts of the body.

"God created women in ways that are amazing. You'll see what I mean as we talk about how menstruation really takes place. Menstruation actually starts in your brain. The pituitary gland at the base of your brain sends a signal to the ovaries to start preparing your body so you can someday become a mother."

"Will I get my period only when I am older then?"

"No, your body will start working at getting your periods soon, even though you should not become a mother until you're married. Your body is just getting ready now. There are tiny egg cells called ovum that have been in your ovaries since you were born, but they were waiting until after puberty to mature. One ovum will mature each month during your fertile years—from about age twelve or thirteen until around age fifty. Each month when the egg cell is mature, it's released from the ovary and travels slowly through the Fallopian tube toward the uterus.

"At the same time the ovum is maturing in the ovary, a blood-filled lining thickens in the uterus as future nourishment for a possible new baby. Each month that a woman does not become pregnant, the egg cell passes through the uterus and dissolves, and it will never become a baby. Then the blood-filled lining gently passes out of the body through the vagina. This is the process called menstruation.

"Now you know what's happening on the inside before you may notice any brown or red spotting on your underwear. It takes about three to seven days each month for the menstrual flow to exit the body. During that time, you can wear a sanitary pad to absorb the flow as it slowly comes out."

"Will you show me how to use this pad?"

"Absolutely! A sanitary pad is made of highly absorbent cotton and other materials, including a lining that keeps the blood from leaking. Most pads have a sticky adhesive strip covered by a tape that you remove just before placing the sticky side down in the middle section of your underpants. The soft side faces you and absorbs your menstrual flow."

"How much blood is there, Mom?"

"In total, it's only a few teaspoons of fluid, but there may sometimes be some clotting, too. And it comes out very slowly, so it will not feel uncomfortable once you get used to it."

"Does it hurt to have your period, Mom?"

"Not really. It just feels slippery or wet, but the pad will absorb it right away. You change your pad every few hours when you go to the bathroom so bacteria does not develop."

"I'm not sure I want that to happen in me. I'm a little afraid to get my period."

"There's no need to be afraid of getting your first period. You may want to keep a sanitary pad in your purse or backpack when you see other signs of puberty start."

"I heard that Talia has bad cramps during her period."

"Sometimes a girl can have cramps when the uterine muscles are contracting. Eating the right natural foods and getting all your proper vitamins and minerals will help reduce that possibility."

"What if I get my period at school?"

"All women have a quiet understanding of what that's like, so your teacher, the school secretary, or school nurse always keep sanitary supplies in their drawer just in case a girl gets surprised by her period coming."

"Will it be messy?"

"Not really, and you'll learn how to manage that very quickly since you get smarter and more responsible every year. When you remove the pad from your underwear, fold it so that all the blood is inside and not showing. Then wrap it up and throw it away. In case some blood goes off the pad and gets on your underwear, a little cold water will keep the stain from setting. Next time we go to the drugstore together—just the two of us—we can look at the different sizes and shapes of sanitary pads."

"Will I know ahead of time?"

"After your first period, you'll usually menstruate every four weeks. You can keep a calendar and mark the days when you have your period. After you see how many days your regular menstrual cycle is, you can start predicting your next period on the calendar—and sometimes you'll even be able to predict what times of the month you will be in a good mood."

"How do you do that, Mom?"

"There are different hormones working in your body at different times of the month. You may want to chart on your calendar when you are feeling happiest and when you are more tired or irritable. That way you can plan bigger projects like your science fair report during those middle days of the cycle and read a good book near the end of the cycle when you may need time to be more calm and relaxed.

"One more thing you need to know is how to dispose of sanitary napkins. They should never be flushed down the toilet, or they will plug it up. When you're away from home, use those small containers in the bathroom slots meant for sanitary supplies. When we're at home, I will show you which wastebasket to use. You can wrap up the used pad first in the plastic wrapper it came in. And always wash your hands afterward."

Choose a time later on when you think it's appropriate to tell your daughter about tampons and how they're used.

Questions to Discuss with Your Daughter:

- How does puberty begin?
- What signs of puberty are you already experiencing? How are you responding to the changes?
- What is the womb? What does it mean to pray, "Blessed is the fruit of your womb?"
- Why is the womb a sacred place?
- Why is modesty important?
- What modesty guidelines should you follow when shopping for clothes or bathing suits?

Let us pray: Thank You, God for creating me, a woman. Help me to always cherish, respect, and accept my body as a beautiful gift from You. Help me to always speak the truth of love with every action of my feminine body.

For Parents with Boys at Puberty

Teaching your son about puberty is simpler for most parents than teaching your daughter. Aside from the moral aspects, boys need to be warned about learning to manage their emotions and have some preparation so as not to be surprised by their first wet dream. The following is a possible conversation to open the topics.

"As you get older, it's good for you to remember some tips on how to manage the changes coming up during puberty. For physical changes, you need to take care of your body by eating the right foods, getting enough sleep, and keeping your body safe and clean. Those are some decisions you should start making on your own, and Mom and I shouldn't have to nag you or remind you. It's time to take some responsibility for yourself."

"Okay, Dad, but can you still remind me sometimes?"

"Sure, Son, I will remind you whenever you need me to. That's part of being a dad, kind of like your coach for life stuff. I'll be here for you through all these changes as you grow up. As your hormones change, some of your moods and emotions could take you by surprise. You might feel confused, irritable, angry, or sad, and you don't know why."

"What can I do about that if that's the way I feel?"

"Well, Son, we must learn to *think* before we *act*, and not just act how we feel. That's why God gave us brains . . . to think. He also gives us virtues to practice over and over until they become good habits."

"You mean like self-control?"

"You've got it, Son. You can practice self-control in your words and actions, no matter what your moods or emotions are. If you feel like hitting someone, you still know you shouldn't. If you feel like saying something nasty or disrespectful, find an appropriate physical way to burn off that anger. Just like the self-discipline you use in sports, you can manage your moods as well. That's self-control. When you experience spiritual changes, whether they're new, deeper thoughts, or temptations, you need to stay close to God by growing in your prayer life and by receiving God's graces by frequent participation in the sacraments."

"You know I already do that, Dad."

"Yes, and I'm proud of you for that, Son. There's something else you need to know before you enter puberty, and it has to do with your reproductive system. The reproductive organs in a boy are his penis, testicles, and scrotum [see diagram].

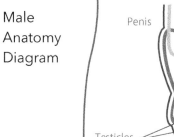
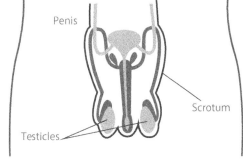

Male Anatomy Diagram

Penis

Scrotum

Testicles

"As God prepares your body to become a man, hormone changes will make your body start to develop sperm cells and a liquid called semen that carries them. These are the cells that will allow you to become a father someday. Sperm are made inside the testes. When your body is figuring out how to do that, some excess sperm and semen may come out of your penis during the night when you're sleeping. Don't worry, it's much different than when you accidentally wet your bed when you were a little kid. Since this semen flow naturally occurs when you're sleeping or dreaming, it's often called a 'wet dream' or nocturnal emission. Those nocturnal emissions will stop when you grow up and your body and hormones get regulated. Just learn how to change your bed sheets on your own, and no one else in the house even needs to know when it happens."

"Dad, what about those other times when my penis gets stiff?"

"A spontaneous erection for a boy is normal and nothing to worry about. It may occur from being stressed out or bored, or waking up, or excited, or for no reason at all. It's not wrong when that happens. It will go away on its own, sometimes with help from a relaxing walk or jog, or even with a cold shower. It's only wrong when you do something intentionally to make an erection occur or to prolong the erection, like rubbing your penis or rubbing yourself up against something. Remember when you were little and we taught you to do something else instead of touching yourself there?"

"Yes, I do, but now it feels different."

"Yes, that's true, but to rub yourself there now would be a sin. It is called masturbation, which is intentionally trying to stir up feelings that are meant for your future wife. God designed those feelings to help you develop a bond with her, not for you to become more selfish. It's wrong to use those feelings for your own pleasure."

"But I know other guys who do it."

"It's a common sin, Son, but one we want to avoid. Masturbation is a selfish activity that can lead to selfish use of your sexual powers; it can even harm your future marriage. If it has already become a habit, we can work on a plan to eliminate it from your life and replace it with a healthy habit that burns some of your sexual tensions during these years of rising testosterone levels. Your faithfulness to your vocation begins right now as you enter manhood. Whether you're going to get married or become a priest, or even if you stay single, you need to be faithful to God's purpose for your body. It's important to stay close to God in daily prayer, weekly Mass, and regular confession. Pray that you will know the vocation God has planned for you."

"I have no clue what that is going to be yet!"

"Always feel free to talk to me about the challenges of growing up and becoming a pure and faithful Christian man. It's not always easy in today's world. To grow in spiritual strength, make daily choices to become a man of virtue, beginning today. A virtuous life will make you a happier man. To grow in physical strength, offer to help with some of the difficult jobs around the house that require more muscle. Do all that you can to grow in body and soul so that you can be a man who is *strong*, *smart*, and *pure*."

"That's plenty to talk for now, Dad. Can we go out and play kickball?"

"I'd be happy to. Let's go!"

Parents Should Decide How Much Information to Give about the Opposite Sex at This Time

When there is a large family with many siblings of both genders, parents may approach the differences and changes between boys and girls more casually. Children also may exhibit differences in curiosity level or intelligence, leading parents to provide information earlier or later.

Children might need only information about their own changes. On the other hand, if boys have sisters in the house or are aware of their mother's menstrual cycle, it is a good time to explain the wonder and beauty of the way God made us. Most importantly, they need to know to respect and be extra kind to women when they have their period.

Some boys at this age may be grossed out at hearing about menstruation, so parents might need to wait a year or two to teach them about it. Other boys may know about menstruation already if they have observed their mother in the bathroom when they were small or found her sanitary supplies and asked about them.

Here's how a conversation might go with your son about menstruation:

"Kyle, let's do something extra nice to surprise mom this weekend."

"Why, Dad? It's not her birthday or anything."

"I know, but she's feeling a little bit tired and sad. That can happen to women for a few days each month at the end of their menstrual cycle."

"What's a menstrual cycle, Dad?"

"It's God's way of preparing a woman's body for motherhood each month."

"Are you going to have another new baby?"

"No, a woman only has her period on the months she is not pregnant."

"So what do you mean by 'a period?' I've heard girls talk about that before."

"Each month, a woman's body builds up a blood-filled lining in her uterus. During each monthly cycle that she does not get pregnant, the blood slowly drips out for about five days, and then it stops."

"I was wondering what that was. Is that what those pads are for on the TV ads?"

"Exactly, Son; those pads absorb the blood flow during her period."

"They get that every month?"

"Yes, from the time they're about thirteen until they are about fifty years old. It's part of their monthly hormone cycle."

"Do boys get something like that, too?"

"No, boys don't have a monthly cycle. But, back to the original topic—that's the time for us to be nicer to Mom. Real men are kind to women all month long, but we can be especially nice and helpful during the days they have their period."

"Yeah, let's think of something she likes."

If your child discovers more information, or is curious and asks questions, answer them simply and truthfully. If you think there is a need for additional conversation, take some private time with your child so you have a chance to bring up the subject.

How Much Does My Child Need to Know About the Marriage Act at This Age?

After children reach puberty, they should have a general understanding that it takes a man and a woman and an act of physical union to create a child. We don't want a girl to be afraid that she could get pregnant by kissing or by chance, and we don't want her taken advantage of by others. We don't want our sons to play with their private parts and disrespect their sexual powers, nor do we want them to use another person for pleasure without knowing that these powers are reserved for marriage. However, the description you give them concerning sexual information will depend on their level of innocence, what they have been exposed to already, and their level of curiosity.

Many fifth and sixth graders are still in the years of innocence, yet many others are beginning puberty. This is one reason why facts about the marriage act should not be taught in the classroom. Other reasons for that topic being taught within the family are modesty, privacy, and the differing levels of curiosity. The Church teaches us that those "intimate details, both biological and effective,"[15] must be presented within the family. It's important that parents decide what information is appropriate for their children at this stage of maturity, but parents also should be aware that they may already be exposed to more than the parents realize.

Parents should try to find out what their children already know. Today's culture is bombarded with sexual messages, so very few children have not run across sexual information. If you have been silent about it so far, they may hesitate to ask you questions. Some children will file the information away, and some will remain curious about it. Therefore, it would be good to use some of those teachable moments—as you did when they were younger—and fill in more information now.

For example, you might have a conversation like this:

> "Jason said a bad word on the playground today, and he got in trouble."
>
> "Oh, really, was it a toilet word or a sexual word?"
>
> "It was the second one, Mom."
>
> "Did you know what the word was?"
>
> "Yes, but I don't want to say it."
>
> "That's good; I'm glad you don't want to say any bad words. Did you know what that word meant?"
>
> "Sort of."
>
> "Do you want to know what it means?"
>
> "Not really."
>
> "Okay, that's fine with me, but when you hear kids talking indecently, know that they sometimes don't even know what they're talking about. But even if they did have the right information, those private topics should only be discussed with me and Dad—in our family. God has a beautiful plan for men and women that many people don't understand, so they mess it up and turn it into something dirty. One of these days when you're ready, we can talk about the beautiful part of God's plan for marriage."
>
> "Okay, Mom."

Here, the child was not really interested in knowing more, but this lets her know you're open to talking and gives you an opportunity to bring up the topic later.

Some parents might ask, "What is an innocent or indirect description of the conjugal union?"

Many innocent children are quite satisfied with simple answers such as, "There is a private hug or 'holy embrace' that's just for married people, and certain kisses or touches that are only for married people. Those actions are wrong for people who are not married." Or, "A honeymoon is when you get used to getting dressed and undressed in the same bedroom now that you are a new family. We never undress with or show our private parts to anyone else. Unless you are married, no one should ever touch your private parts." You can also say, "The sixth commandment forbids us to touch anyone in a sexual way that is reserved only for his or her husband or wife," and "The ninth commandment requires that we look at others as children of God; we are not to have impure thoughts about them."

Simple and general descriptions respect the dignity and innocence of our children. In some cases, this might be all they need to know until they are eleven or twelve, depending on their exposure to the media and the level of innocence of their friends.

Even very innocent children, however, need to be able to make correct judgments about what is going on around them so they can form their consciences properly. Even if your child has never seen a PG-13 movie, they still may be exposed to messages on billboards, in the grocery store, and in the news. This is the age when they should learn objective standards of right and wrong, creating a healthy moral framework for life. These are times you can use the many teachable moments of life to reinforce God's beautiful plan and help them see the flaws and evil in the contrasting exposure.

For example, you might have a conversation like this:

"I saw that show on TV you were watching. That man and woman were in bed together—are they married?"

"No, Dad, I don't think so."

"Do you think that is the right thing to do, to sleep in the same bed when you aren't married?"

"I don't know."

"Doing that actually shows disrespect for each other rather than love. You know what God teaches us in the sixth commandment, don't you?"

"Yes, 'Thou shall not commit adultery.'"

"Well, that means you should not act like married people when you're not married, and it's wrong for someone to live with his girlfriend when he's not married to her. That is unfair to her, and wrong in the eyes of God, who has a beautiful plan for marriage. Do you know that God has the best plans for all of us because He loves us so much?"

"Yes, I guess so, Dad."

"Well, do you want to follow God's plan?"

"I think so."

"I think you would always want to respect women—and hope that all young men respect your future wife, too."

"I'm not getting married for a long time, Dad."

"Well, we hope you always choose to do the right thing and wait until marriage before you live with someone. That is an important part of God's plan for marriage.

As you practice purity and keeping your thoughts close to God's, you will learn how to see a woman's beauty as something holy, something to be respected. Every beautiful woman does not have to be a temptation to sin, but can instead be an opportunity to appreciate the beauty of God. Only people with a pure heart are truly happy, because they are able to love God and their neighbor and see the goodness of God in them."

At another time, you can add to that information to deepen it:

"When a young man reaches puberty, his hormonal changes spur on a new feeling called the sexual drive. This is a strong attraction to women that was not present when he was a young boy."

"Is that why Michael is so interested in girls?"

"Yes, it is, Son; his body is drawing him slowly into manhood, even though he won't be ready to get married for a long time. God has given men this desire to behold the beauty of a woman and be in awe of her, and this is good. God made women beautiful intentionally, and we should thank Him for that! But it's very important over the next few years to develop your purity of mind and heart so you focus on God's will, not on your own feelings. To begin your purity challenge, you need to practice working on 'custody of the eyes.' Custody of the eyes, or 'purity of vision' as the *Catechism* calls it, is the practice of turning your eyes away from the sight of a woman who is immodestly dressed. Why do men need to do this? Because the sight, sound, or smell of a beautiful woman can take over his imagination and easily lead to lustful thoughts or the idea that she is an object for pleasure."

"I don't look at girls that way, Dad."

"That's a good sign that you are pure, Son. A young man with a pure mind and heart trains himself to see the beauty of a young woman who is made in the likeness and image of God and is a person who deserves respect."

Gradual Information

As a child grows physically, spiritually, and emotionally, the parent should build on the information already discussed. When children enter middle school, you want them to be prepared to avoid or assess the new exposures. They can still be innocent without being ignorant. They will also need to be armed spiritually with prayer and the sacraments. This will keep them focused on their mission to grow as a child of God with true and pure friendships, instead of following the crowd and going the wrong way.

A simple conversation about growing up at God's pace might begin with:

"It's so much fun to see you enjoy being a girl [or boy]. Try not to worry about growing up too quickly. You're growing at God's pace for you. When you're ten, enjoy life as a ten-year-old. When you're thirteen, be as mature as a thirteen-year-old should be. Your most important tasks now are learning to love your family and friends in unselfish ways and learning how to develop real friendships without using people. As you learn about Christian relationships, it's important to remain pure to hear God's will for your vocation. Sometimes you'll see the other kids around you trying to grow up too fast. Remember that you're doing the right thing when you follow God's plan for you, and the sacrifice of being good is always worthwhile. What do you think about growing into an adult?"

Listen to their concerns and respond with understanding and truth. Then you can move the conversation to other positive topics you want them to focus on during their middle school years. Ask them about their interests, tell them about the talents you see them developing, and talk together about their goals, plans, and dreams. And then let them just be kids while they are kids!

The Season of Advent Is a Good Time to Discuss Conception

One of the best times of year to teach about love, life, and the human body is during the weeks leading up to Christmas, during Advent. It's not always necessary to give specific details about the marriage act during this time, but the Gospels open the way for you to discuss it. Be aware of the questions or information in your child's mind.

A simple time to bring this up would be on the feast of the Immaculate Conception, December 8. You can mention the two different topics—one is the Immaculate Conception and the other is the Gospel story of the Annunciation of the Virgin Birth read on that day.

Your teaching could go like this:

"Today we're going to Mass for the feast of the Immaculate Conception. Do you know what we are celebrating?"

"Yes, Dad, that Mary was conceived without original sin."

"Great, Bobby. Today we celebrate the day that Mary was conceived in St. Anne's womb, and from the moment of her conception, she did not inherit original sin like the rest of us."

"Wait, I thought it meant that Mary didn't sin when she conceived Jesus?"

"Well, we all know that Mary never sinned. But lots of people think the Feast of the Immaculate Conception is about the Virgin Birth. It might be confusing because the Gospel reading today is about the Annunciation, which led to the Virgin Birth, another great mystery of our faith. Today's gospel tells of a different event many years after the Immaculate Conception called the Annunciation when Mary was a young teenager. That's when the Angel Gabriel visited her and asked her if she would be the mother of Jesus."

"Sure, I knew that, Dad."

"But back at the Immaculate Conception, when Mary was conceived in her mother's womb, God spared Mary from original sin. The Apostles' Creed says that Jesus was conceived by the Holy Spirit. That's what today's Gospel teaches us. The angel Gabriel appeared to Mary, and as soon as Mary said 'yes' to God, Jesus started to grow in Mary's womb. That's why we pray, 'Blessed is the fruit of your womb' in the Hail Mary. So now you know that these are two different events, but both have to do with conception. The Immaculate Conception was when Mary was created by God in her mother's womb with the cooperation of both of her parents. The Annunciation was when God became flesh by the power of the Holy Spirit, conceived in Mary's womb to become Jesus, Our Savior."

This type of conversation should be had with your child while the younger ones are not around so they have a chance to bring up other related topics they might be curious about. Be calm, be prayerful, and seek the guidance of the Holy Spirit when you give your child simple answers to their questions.

Strong, Smart, and Pure: At Puberty ⟹ Rewind

Strong: As you prepare your children for puberty, you are laying a strong foundation for the meaning of love and the facts of life. Continue to help your preteens become strong in virtue as they learn how their bodies are changing.

Smart: Help your children to be smart about friendships, smart about their faith, smart about their changing bodies, and smart enough to focus on being good and getting a good education. Guiding them through this stage helps you be a smarter parent, too, and prepares you to lead them as they mature. Know that God's love helps you to be patient and calm as you parent your child through puberty.

Pure: Your children still look to you as their first guide, so continuing to set a good example for them and taking advantage of casual "teachable moments" go a long way to helping them remain pure.

Strong, Smart, and Pure: Fast Forward ⟹ To Young Adolescence

Strong: We're moving through puberty toward young adolescence. Exciting, isn't it? Using the resources throughout this book will build your strength and confidence. Remain strong in your faith, your example, your understanding, and your interaction with your children.

Smart: Parents with teenagers can relate to these words of Jesus to His disciples: "I am sending you like sheep in the midst of wolves; so be shrewd as serpents and simple as doves" (Mt 10:16). Your children are more and more out in the world, and the culture and peers may be pressuring them to conform to a different set of unspoken rules. The big news to share with them now is that they can be confident and knowledgeable and still remain virtuous. In fact, they are so smart that they can actually lead others toward God's way of thinking versus the thinking of the confused culture.

Pure: No doubt, this could be a challenging time for your young teen. Trust in God's providence and what you've taught them all along, and they will feel encouraged in their commitment to be pure. It's also good to remember that if there are any mistakes along the way, God is present in the Sacrament of Reconciliation to forgive their sins and assist them in recommitting to purity.

CHAPTER 6

LoveEd for Young Adolescence

> The relationship between a man and a woman is essentially a relationship of love: "Sexuality [which is] oriented, elevated and integrated by love, acquires truly human quality."
>
> —Sacred Congregation for Catholic Education, *Educational Guidance in Human Love*, n. 6

If not you, who will pass on to the next generation God's beautiful plan for conjugal love?

Parents, you are "the light of the world!" Yes, it is your *privilege* to bring new life into the world, and your *responsibility* to teach your children about the power of love and life. Psalm 145:11 says, "They speak of the glory of your reign / and tell of your mighty works." No one can take your place in this sensitive task. You will also find that these discussions of life help forge a bond between you and your child that is the beginning of a more intimate and more adult relationship. You are entrusting to them the truths of life and love, and you are counting on them to receive this information with a holy attitude. This is too important to leave up to the school alone. You are the one to provide your child with the knowledge of one of the most glorious mysteries of God: procreation.

Many parents are challenged by the thought of talking to their son or daughter about human sexuality, especially the conjugal union and conception. This is not an easy conversation to have in an era of confusion and debasement of sexuality.

Some challenges might present themselves in various forms. For example:

- We may wonder what words to say or what examples to use.
- We are not always aware of what our children already know or have heard.
- Sometimes we think they know everything, so we hesitate to bring up the topic.
- We may be unsure how much science or morality they need at this age.
- We may be afraid of appearing old-fashioned, or we may be afraid they will ask us if we remained virgins until we were married.
- It's also possible that we have not completely understood or lived the Catholic teachings in the past, so we are not even convinced we can or should pass on that information.

Yet in your parental heart, you know it is your responsibility to inform your child about these important aspects of life and love. The *LoveEd* program, along with the Church, is here to assist you and give you the confidence to fulfill that responsibility.

This is the time to help your young adolescents know more deeply than ever that they are not alone, that they are part of a bigger story: God's love story! You want them to know that God has a great plan for them to become a loving man or woman. This plan is yet to unfold. The virtue of chastity will give them the best preparation to become a true gift of themselves by showing God's love for others.

Start with the Meaning of Love

You want your children to understand that love is the willingness to sacrifice oneself for the good of others. Love is not simply a feeling. The feeling of romance can lead to love, but it is not love itself. Romantic feelings could be a door to love or a door to sin. In order for romantic feelings to lead to real love, it is imperative that love includes many sacrifices, including the sacrifice of saving oneself for marriage.

Family love and friendship love teach us how to get along well with others and develop the virtues needed to be a lifelong loving person. Making sacrifices in those circles of love in your children's lives now will help them later on in marriage, the single life, or religious life. The habits of virtue will become part of your children, and they begin to see that virtue is its own reward. They will feel good about themselves when they are living right and winning the fight against temptation, even if they feel alone at the moment. Help motivate your teens to choose virtue of their own free will. This is an important part of loving now and loving relationships in their future. The virtue of chastity will build upon the strength of the other virtues they practice.

We Were Created to Love

We are physical beings with God's perfect design. We are not just a spirit planted into a container (a body). When God breathed life (a soul) into the earthly body of Adam, the *whole* person of Adam, body and soul, became alive in the image and likeness of God. We do not just *have* bodies; we *are* persons of bodies and souls. We read in Genesis that our existence as specifically sexual beings, male and female, is good. "Male and female he created them" (Gn 1:27), and then God declared it "very good" (v. 31). To fulfill God's purpose of becoming one flesh in marriage is a way to share God's love with our spouse and our children. This relationship is so important and powerful that it is a sacrament—a living sign of God's love in the world.

Love is our mission as Christians; we are meant to be living signs of God's love in the world.

To live this well, parents must continue to teach concepts of self-mastery, love-giving and life-giving, selflessness, and gift of self. Guide your adolescents to embrace a Christian vision of life and love and help them to understand the importance of purity of mind and heart. Explain that practicing chastity in all their friendships and romantic relationships is part of the call to holiness and respect for the dignity of persons. They should learn how to be aware of and avoid those occasions that might be a temptation to sin.

Develop Your Talents So You Can Be a Gift of Love

Adolescence is a time for teens to get to know themselves, as well as their strengths and weaknesses. Your children should be challenging themselves daily to grow their talents, study hard, work hard, and play hard. As they learn more about themselves, they begin to see what God might be calling them to do as adults. This is one of the ways they become a gift of love to the world. They can be loving persons in all their relationships and in their choice of vocation and occupation.

Many service occupations lend themselves to becoming a gift of love to others, such as teaching, nursing, developing a business that serves others and employs others, serving the public good through safety or protection, law or medicine, building construction, and so on. As your teens grow, remind them that they are to be gifts of love to both their future families and the whole of society.

The Facts of Life in the Context of God's Love

At adolescence, additional information should be given to teens about their own anatomy as well as that of the opposite sex. They should hear from you about the importance of marriage, how a child is conceived, how a baby grows in the mother's womb, and why Catholics respect life from the moment of conception. Teach them God's plan for these gifts He has given us and how to use them properly in marriage.

Using the Scriptures to Teach Your Child the Facts of Life and Virginity

If your child has reached puberty and young adolescence and you have still not discussed with him or her about how babies are conceived, it's important to have that conversation even if your child says he or she already knows it. This will also help you find out what other messages your child is taking in or any misinformation he or she may have.

The *LoveEd* videos teach the anatomy and science behind love, marriage, and life. If you wish to discuss these topics at some time before viewing the video, or review the facts sometime after viewing the video, it might be helpful to use stories from Scripture and our Catholic faith as a platform for discussion.

For example, you can bring up the topic in a comfortable way by mentioning the feast of the Immaculate Conception. This introduces these teachings in a sacred setting, beginning with a topic your children may already know about. Advent, Christmas, or the feast of the Annunciation could create perfect opportunities.

Perhaps the conversation might go like this:

> "December 8 is the feast of Mary's Immaculate Conception, but that day's Gospel is about the Virgin Birth. Do you know that those two things are very different events?"
>
> "I never thought about it."
>
> "You know what original sin is, right?"
>
> "Yes, the sin we all inherited from Adam and Eve."

"I'm glad you know that. Did you know that everyone born inherited original sin except two people?"

"Well, Jesus didn't since He was God and couldn't sin."

"Yes, that's true, and the other person was Mary, the mother of Jesus. And do you know what conception means?"

"When a baby starts growing in the mother's womb."

"See, you are smart about this stuff. So the Immaculate Conception is when Mary began to grow as a tiny baby in her mom's womb. Her mom was St. Anne and her dad was St. Joachim. And from the instant Mary was conceived, God freed her from original sin, so she had no tendency to sin to tarnish her soul. Since God knows everything, He knew Mary would say yes to being the mother of His Son, Jesus, so He made her conceived without sin."

"So why isn't that Gospel about Anne and Joachim finding out they were going to have baby Mary?"

"Good question! Maybe nobody wrote that down since they didn't know at that time the day would be a future feast!"

"I get it, and we celebrate Mary's birthday on September 8, nine months from now."

"Yes, and this Immaculate Conception of Mary is such an amazing privilege from God that we celebrate December 8 as a feast day in the Church."

"So that's why we have to go to Mass on that day?"

"Yes, we choose to go, as another reason to celebrate our amazing faith."

If that was a bit much for your child, wait until a later time to discuss the Gospel story of the Virgin Birth. If he or she seems interested and wants more information right now, move ahead.

"Let's read together the Gospel from Luke 2:1-7 in our Bible. This is the story of the Virgin Birth, meaning that Mary gave birth to Jesus while she was still a virgin. We also believe that Mary remained a virgin throughout her life. You know how when we pray the Creed, we always say that Jesus was 'conceived by the Holy Spirit'? This is the Gospel passage that explains how that happened. Go ahead and read it aloud for us."

"'In the sixth month the angel Gabriel was sent from God to a city of Galilee named Nazareth. To a virgin betrothed to a man whose name was Joseph, of the house of David, and the virgin's name was Mary.'"

"Let's stop there first. Have you heard about the angel Gabriel before?"

"Yes, he is one of God's messengers."

"That's right. Do you know what a virgin is?"

"Well, I've heard it in a song before, but I'm not exactly sure."

"A virgin is a person who is pure, both spiritually and physically, and stays focused on God's will for his or her soul and body. The definition of virgin also includes a person who is not married and has never had sexual relations with anyone, pretty much meaning that they have never slept together."

"Oh."

"Do you know what "betrothed" means in that Bible verse?"

"Does it mean that Mary and Joseph were engaged to be married?"

"Yes, that's right; you got it. Now read the next verse."

"'And he came to her and said, "Hail, full of grace, the Lord is with you!" But she was greatly troubled at the saying, and considered in her mind what sort of greeting this might be.'"

"How do you think you would feel if an angel appeared to you?"

"I might not be sure it was an angel, but I might be worried, like Mary, too."

"So now read the next verse."

"'Do not be afraid, Mary, for you have found favor with God.' That would be a good thing to hear from God, to know that He likes me."

"Well, God does like you—He loves you more than you can imagine! Let's read on, since next comes the part that even confuses Mary."

"'Behold, you will conceive in your womb and bear a son, and you shall name him Jesus. He will be great and will be called Son of the Most High.'"

"This is the part that puzzled Mary because she knew she wasn't married yet to Joseph, and she knew you were supposed to be married to have a baby. So read what she said to the angel in verse thirty-four."

"'How can this be, since I have no relations with a man?'"

"Even though she was an innocent virgin, Mary knew that it takes a man and a woman to conceive a baby. And she knew she hadn't had relations with Joseph that could make her pregnant. So then the angel explained to her in the next verse how this could happen."

"'The Holy Spirit will come upon you, and the power of the Most High will overshadow you. Therefore the child to be born will be called holy, the Son of God.'"

"Now skip down to verse thirty-eight. Even though Mary might have been surprised by this announcement, she responded right away with her yes to God."

"'Mary said, "Behold, I am the handmaid of the Lord. May it be done to me according to your word."' I have heard that part before, when we prayed the Angelus prayer."

"Yes, the Angelus prayer is taken right from this Gospel. So this is how Jesus was conceived by the Holy Spirit as we say in the Apostles Creed. And this is what we celebrate in the feast of the Annunciation on March 25."

"Oh, I get it now, March 25 is nine months before Christmas."

"Yes, I knew you'd get that part."

"Of course I would."

"Now, everyone else besides Adam and Eve and Jesus comes from two parents, one human mother and one human father. Jesus was the only person born who didn't have a human father. God the Holy Spirit actually conceived Jesus, and Jesus grew for nine months in Mary's womb."

If this is enough for your child, you can stop or take a break. When you reintroduce the subject, whether it is a day, week, or month later, you can say:

"Remember when we talked about the way that Jesus was conceived by the Holy Spirit?"

"Yes."

"Do you know how you were conceived?"

"You told me when I was younger that God planned me to grow in mom's womb from a tiny egg cell. Is that true?"

"Yes, it is true, and that was all the detail you needed then to see how awesome God is. But there is a little bit more that you need to know now that you are growing from a girl into a woman (or boy into a man). It's something the Blessed Virgin Mary knew when the angel appeared to her, and it's something you need to know to make sense of your growing womanhood (or manhood)."

"Okay, what is it?"

"It's how those sexual relations are part of love-giving and life-giving in marriage."

"Do I need to know that now? I think I already know."

"Yes, you need to hear it from me in the right way. Although Jesus was conceived when the Holy Spirit miraculously overshadowed Mary, all the rest of us were conceived with the cooperation of a man and a woman in an act designed by God. Let's go to the Bible again, this time, way in the beginning in the Book of Genesis, chapters 1 and 2. Read verse twenty-seven first."

"'God created mankind in his image; / in the image of God he created them; / male and female he created them.'"

"That tells us a couple things; one is that God created us in two sexes—male and female—and we are both created in the image of God with His dignity."

"I know that already."

"Great, now read verse twenty-eight so we can hear what God asked the male and female to do."

"'God blessed them and God said to them: Be fertile and multiply; fill the earth and subdue it.'"

"First God says that He blesses the male and female and our ability to have children—that's what fertility is. Then He tells us to "multiply" and have more children so we can fill up the earth with His blessings."

"Is that why there are so many people in the world, because we are all blessings from God? And what about all that empty space in Texas and Nebraska and Wyoming? Do we have to fill that up, too?"

"Well, we all need to do our best to fill the world with God's love. Let's move to Genesis 2:24-25 to find out what God says about how the man and woman are to be fruitful to fill up the earth."

"'That is why a man leaves his father and mother and clings to his wife, and the two of them become one body. The man and his wife were both naked, yet they felt no shame.'"

"Here are some important instructions about conceiving new life. First God says to leave your father and mother—which means to get married and start a new family. Next, He says that the man then cleaves to his wife, which means that he stays close to her and faithful forever, and third, God says the two shall become one flesh."

"I think I know what you mean, Dad (or Mom). But you know people do that when they are not married."

"Let me tell you how it is supposed to be in marriage. After the wedding, the couple goes off alone together, and they are so happy to be together. As I mentioned when you were younger, on their honeymoon, they get comfortable getting undressed and dressed in the same bedroom together so they are not embarrassed. But there is more than that. They can now sleep together, hug and kiss, and get so close together that their bodies can actually join together in a way that is blessed by God. It is called the marriage act, or sexual intercourse. Some people refer to this act as 'sex' or 'making love.' The Bible calls it 'becoming one flesh.' During that special loving time, the husband can have an erection of his penis and the wife's vagina prepares to receive him. The husband can then gently place his penis in his wife's vagina so that his sperm cells can be transferred into her body. If an egg cell is present in the woman that day, his sperm and her egg cell can join together and become a new baby. That joining of the sperm and egg cell is called conception.

This is the way God has planned for all people to be conceived: in an act of love between husband and wife. A couple doesn't get pregnant every time they make love—only if an egg cell is present that day in the woman. Even so, this union is a blessing from God for married couples to enjoy one another in a specifically married way. Notice in the Bible that making love is only blessed after marriage, not before. Before marriage, it is a sin to sleep together with the person you love because God designed sexual intercourse to draw married couples closer together so they can stay together and raise all their children with love. That's how God created the sexuality of man and woman to be holy. Does that make sense to you?"

"Okay, I knew some of that, but not the holy part. All I remember is that you told me not to look at the people on TV without clothes on."

"Yes, because that television show is about using someone's body in a wrong way. The marriage act is private and loving between the husband and wife."

"Do I have to know anything else?"

"Do you want to know anything else?"

"No, let me think about all this for a while."

"Let me know if you have any questions, and we can do the next lesson some other time, okay?"

"Okay, thanks."

The Marriage Act Explained in a Sacred Way

The *LoveEd* video and the list of definitions in this chapter can help you teach your preteen or teen about the marriage act (sexual intercourse). Some children will want to know more details when the topic is at hand, and others may choose to let that science sink into their minds before placing it within a context that is beyond their understanding. Since children have not experienced the sexual passion of an adult, they sometimes hear about the mechanics of sexual intercourse and cannot imagine how it can be beautiful. This is where another simple yet sacred description (as in the above Scripture dialogue) can help them see the marriage act as part of God's beautiful plan. Emphasize for them the importance of following God's plan for the sacredness of the marriage act. Within marriage, God blesses this union; outside of marriage, the act of sexual intercourse is a serious sin that mocks God's plan. Help them see that, while they wait for their wedding night, the loving desires they have can be channeled into doing good and kind things for others, resisting the temptation to use these sexual powers in a selfish or immoral way.

The Truth About Sexual Desires

Explain to your child that, beginning at puberty and adolescence, young men will experience an increased attraction to women; this is called the sexual drive and is due to an increase in the hormone testosterone. Young women, with an increase in the hormone estrogen, also have a heightened desire to love and be loved. In giving them this warning, your children will not be surprised when new feelings occur, and they will know that they are designed by God to manage their behavior when they feel these emotions.

You can explain this to young teens by using examples of other desires in their lives that they have learned to manage. Their desire to eat candy all the time has been managed because they may have learned that too much candy makes them sick. The tantrums they used to display as a two-year-old have hopefully turned into a more mature way of communicating frustration. They are probably learning how to manage their time between schoolwork, family time, and recreation. Sexual desires can be managed, too, with good habits of self-control and patience while they integrate the knowledge of the true purpose and meaning of human sexual expression. A sign that your teen is growing in maturity is that he or she can manage his or her behavior toward what is right and good. This also includes the humility to admit and confess one's mistakes and sins, as well as to be able to pick oneself up after a failure.

Why Wait?

The dignity of men and women and the dignity of marriage are harmed by sexual sin.

A fulfilling sexual relationship requires a lifetime of faithfulness and exclusivity. Our human nature is designed in such a way that we want to love and be loved. God's plan for man and woman in marriage includes a lifetime of love—a passionate, committed love affair that lasts fifty, sixty, or seventy years, through good times and bad. That can include all the poems and flowers and candy and romance that are added to that diamond ring, as well as the many years raising the children born of their love. In that context, men and women can become the persons God wants them to be. Their virtues are practiced daily; their dignity is respected. They are known to one another in only those ways that join them to God.

This fulfilling outcome can never happen in a one-night stand, a trial sexual relationship, or a temporary affair. Sin divides people while love unites them. Losing one's virginity in casual relationships can lead to heartaches and physical diseases. Virginity is the gift you give only once: on your wedding night. Virginity before marriage is the beginning of marital faithfulness. Do all that you can to encourage your teens to live purely so they will have no regrets later on. Self-respect is something they never want to lose. Sacrificing their desires now will pay off later in marriage.

Help your teens understand why sexual sin is offensive to the dignity of the marriage act and harmful to their future marriage. As the years progress, make sure they understand at various stages of their development why sexual sins are harmful: immodest behavior and dress, misuse of the Internet, pornography and indecent entertainment, masturbation, sexting, premarital sex, cohabitation, and abortion. Help them learn what is wrong about artificial contraception, homosexual acts, sexual abuse, and the use of illicit reproductive technologies. All of these are explained in the *Catechism of the Catholic Church*.

You can also find teen-friendly explanations to read with your young teen in the *Parent's Guide of Love & Life: A Christian Sexual Morality Guide for Teens* by this same author (see www.sexrespect.com).

It Helps to Understand the Purpose of Obedience

The teachings in *LoveEd* are rooted in the reality of God's love: that God loves us with a passion, and we are called to love God in return and to share His love with others. Jesus taught, "Love God with your whole heart, mind, will and strength. And love your neighbor as yourself" (see Mk 12:31). Children and teens need to be taught how to love in the environment of their homes, their friendships, and in the romantic circles that can lead to a lifelong, loving marriage that is open to life. Being rooted in love throughout their growing years should help your preteens and teens understand that chastity and purity prepare them for true love in their future and an eternal love with God.

It's very beneficial to teach your teens the purpose of sexual morality and chastity. However, obeying the teachings will also help them grow into their understanding. Whether or not they understand it all now, any sexual sins they may commit will eventually have consequences for themselves or their future marriage. Since consequences could be serious (sexually transmitted infection, sterility, a selfish habit of using others, an inability to trust someone who abandoned them, or guilt associated with the sexual act), it is best to prevent them from happening. Your children did not understand electricity when you taught them not to stick their fingers in the electric outlet, nor did they understand the theory of motion when you taught them not to run into the street chasing their kickball, but they now live because they obeyed. As the saying goes, "God always forgives, Mankind sometimes forgives, and Nature never forgives."

We Choose How Our Sexual Passions Will Be Directed

Each person chooses the direction of his or her focus of sexual energy: toward selfishness or toward loving one's spouse in marriage. Lust or love?

The selfish use of sexual passions is called lust, one of the seven capital sins. Lust destroys love. Lust is not a preparation for love. Lust is using others or yourself for pleasure. Lust, even in marriage, can harm the relationship because, deep down inside, the person feels used instead of loved. Thus, their sexual experience divides the couple instead of uniting them. How many women feel used by their partner for sex rather than cherished and treasured? Anyone can feel the emptiness in their heart when they are being used.

Passionate love directed toward one's spouse and family, which is selfless, faithful, and open to life, is the path to a beautiful and real love. Passionate love is great, like the love of Jesus, and always seeks the good of the other person, whether that is enacted in abstinence or the marriage act. Resistance to sexual temptation keeps love pure and is central to any loving relationship and any kind of humane society.

Love Versus Lust

Love grows.	Lust kills.
Love is giving.	Lust is using.
Love is caring for others first.	Lust is selfish.
Love helps others grow.	Lust hurts others' growth.
Love is generous.	Lust is demanding.
Love brings joy.	Lust brings temporary thrills that lead to secrets and lies.
Love sees the inner beauty.	Lust looks to the external shell.
Love builds the relationship.	Lust is a harmful substitute for people without good relationships.
Love brings unity.	Lust is divisive.

Some kids might ask, "When I see an attractive person and I like him/her, is that always lust?" No. Thanking God for the beauty of women or the attractiveness of men is different than lust. Lust is stirring up of sexual desires that are not at the service of God and are not life-giving. It's unfortunate today that our popular culture designs most of its entertainment for the purpose of stirring up lust in anyone who will pay attention. Today, it is all the more important that Christian young men and women are alert to these temptations and prepared to resist them. To resist a lustful thought toward a woman, envision her as someone's wife, sister, or mother someday, and pray that she fulfills her vocation. Look for the good and beauty of her personhood, and try not to let her physical attractiveness cause your desires to be out of control.

Sexual Integrity

Catholic teaching on human sexuality leads us to wholeness and the knowledge of real love. Sexual integrity is the capacity to use our free will to manage our sexual impulses according to God's plan for love as a man or as a woman. Sexual integrity is also referred to as sexual wholeness, meaning that we accept ourselves as the whole person God created us to be and live according to His design. Sexual integrity requires the virtue of chastity, which is the spiritual energy God gives us to place our sexual desires at the service of God's plan for us, whether married or celibate. When we practice sexual integrity, our love becomes pure and a better reflection of God's love. To grow in sexual integrity, we need to be ready to manage our behaviors and resist temptation.

Resisting Temptation

Certain video games, magazines, movies, or websites invite people to sin against purity by presenting indecent pictures or scenes that can imprint themselves on their subconscious memory. This is a serious invitation to sin where the devil can take hold. It is important to *run* as far away as possible from Satan and his vices. All of these temptations or questionable situations are to be avoided when practicing purity.

How can you help your teens to know what to do when temptation lurks? Instruct them to get out of the situation, say a prayer, or think of their favorite sports or other interests when faced with a difficult situation. When watching TV, they can become quicker with the remote control in order to change channels when commercials or shows become impure or indecent. And the temptations are not just on TV either. There are plenty of impure web pop-ups and sites to avoid on the Internet and other places. Teens might need to avoid going to certain stores or places of recreation that could become places of temptation.

St. Catherine of Siena fought a battle with lust in a time when it was scandalous for a woman to admit such a temptation. One day, when she seemed tempted beyond her strength, she cried out to the Lord for more help. The Lord appeared to her the next morning, and she said to him, "Where were you when my soul and mind were filled with terrible thoughts?"

The Lord paused. "Did you enjoy them?" He asked.

"Why no, of course not," she replied.

"Did you fight against them?"

She replied, "Why, yes, with all my strength."

"Dear daughter, can't you see? I was always with you. For the strength you found, you found in me."

Dangers of Alcohol and Drugs to Decision Making

Teach teens the dangers of drinking alcohol, especially how alcohol can affect their ability to make good, moral decisions. The first thing that shuts down while under the influence of alcohol is the inhibition against sin. The instinct and desire for pleasure and comfort can override a well-formed conscience when it is not working. Many people have lost their virginity after a couple glasses of wine or beer and regret what they did the next day. Teach teens how to avoid all occasions of sin, especially those that have long-term consequences.

Dangers of Pornography

Even though you've taught your child that porn is to be avoided, be aware that many young teens have already seen some porn. Some are already addicted to pornography's stimulus to the pleasure center in the brain. If you suspect that may be true, please get them the help needed to break that habit immediately. All is not lost. There are numerous Catholic agencies helping people break this addiction.

Even if your young teen has never viewed pornography, more safety precautions must be internalized by your teen to help him or her avoid porn when no one is looking. Teens need to be aware that pornography is no longer something people sneak around and look for in a magazine or an X-rated film, as in years past. Pornography is coming after you to trap you. It can come at you through the Internet, even when you are searching for something good. Unfortunately, it can even get through the porn filters you hopefully have on your computers, so it is worth the price to buy the strongest filters you can.

God wants us to see His beauty in others. God programmed our bodies physically and chemically so that sexual passion within marriage is good, whereas selfish use of sex is harmful. We cannot change the way He made us, but we can direct all our sexual desires toward good. Viewing pornography is a detour on the road to sexual health and goodness. Pornography is not about love at all, whether outside or inside marriage.

Continue to give your teen the support and tools he or she needs to keep his or her mind pure from the lure of pornography. Those who make billions of dollars from advertising on porn websites do not care at all about your teen's sexual health.

Love Versus Porn

Love cares about the person.	Pornography does not care about the person.
Love uplifts the person.	Pornography degrades the dignity of the person.
Love is bonding with another.	Pornography is bonding with fictitious pictures.
Love is merciful and kind.	Pornography hurts the people in it and those who use it.
Love is beautiful.	Pornography is ugly.
Love focuses on the virtues.	Pornography is only about the body.
Love is fulfilling.	Pornography is empty.
Love is freeing.	Pornography is addicting.
Love is real.	Pornography is fake.
Love is a reflection of God.	Pornography keeps people from seeking and experiencing the real love they deserve and need. Pornography is a counterfeit attempt at sexual pleasure that does not lead to love.

Discussing Homosexuality With Your Adolescent

Our society's views on same-sex attraction (SSA) have changed radically in the last twenty years. Some people feel that homosexuality is fine because they want everyone to have what they desire and they don't understand God's plan for marital union. There can be genuine kindness and compassion to this thinking, and we all should certainly have compassion for everyone, regardless of their sexual inclinations. As Catholics, we have compassion for people who struggle with SSA or any other struggle. We love them and accept them without judgment, but we cannot accept homosexual acts as part of God's plan. We know this from the Old and New Testament and from consistent Church teaching over two thousand years. We know this from natural law as well. Despite our culture's relatively recent acceptance of gay "marriage," God's definition of marriage does not change since it was written within the human body at the creation of the male and female persons.

The appropriate age to discuss homosexuality will depend on your child's exposure. If a child is not exposed to homosexual relationships, the Church suggests waiting until adolescence to discuss it. At a young age, parents can simply state that persons of the same sex cannot be married in the Church because God designed us so that each baby has one mother and one father. That is a true statement according to the science of conception, and it may be all the information your child needs at that time.

At the ages of puberty and adolescence, teach your preteens or teens first about the science and theology of the natural marriage union and pregnancy so they can see the goodness of God's plan before you explain to them the social and moral problems of homosexuality.

The science of the marriage act very clearly teaches us that the marriage union, the act of sexual intercourse, can only occur between a man and a woman because they have opposite sexual organs. Two people with the same sexual organs cannot unite those organs, because their bodies were not designed to unite. This may raise additional questions from a young adolescent who is well aware that today's culture promotes same-sex unions and homosexual "marriage."

But the consummation of a marriage is a physical renewal of the marriage vows. The husband and wife give themselves to one another in a loving physical embrace that is both unitive and open to the possibility of creating new life. Any same-sex attempt at union is futile because it is not anatomically possible, so it is not unitive, nor procreative. Thus, an act of same-sex sexual pleasuring is not the marriage act. Even if the sexual organs are used in a homosexual act, the act is not designed to be fulfilling to the human heart and soul; it cannot satisfy, and requires more and more empty gratification as it continues seeking the fulfillment of love it desires. Gratifying feelings of sexual pleasure are not the same as sexual fulfillment. The efforts to seek sexual pleasure with a person of the same sex are forms of mutual masturbation; they are attempts to unite the reproductive system to the digestive system. Neither constitutes a true union of a couple's sexual organs. The natural meaning of the marriage union is for unity and procreation, which is fulfilling the needs of the human person. The organs are called the genitals because they are made to *generate* life. Neither union nor procreation is possible in a same-sex union. It cannot truly fulfill physical needs, nor express a love that lives on in a whole new person. Gratification is at a physical level and, even when repeated over and over, cannot reach human fulfillment.

God's plan for marriage includes a man and a woman, united in love, faithful to one another and a total self-gift of one to the other. Substitutes for God's plan do not fulfill the needs of the human heart. Although two people of the same gender may truly love one another as genuine friends, it is dishonest to say that they can act in the physical way that God designed for a married man and woman. Friendships of people the same sex must be celibate in order for their actions to be considered having sexual integrity.

The Church is sympathetic and compassionate toward people who have same-sex attraction (SSA) and calls them to live a life of chastity in order to be fulfilled in their relationship with Christ; the Church also offers pastoral support.[16] Persons with SSA can lead a good and holy life, as do many single and celibate heterosexual people. The Church offers support groups, such as www.couragerc.org, for people with SSA who are struggling to live a chaste life. Teach your preteens or teens that each person has a different struggle in life, and no one who is different should be made fun of or left out.

Gender Confusion

Gender identity and other issues related to our sexuality are being debated in the culture as never before. How do we understand these issues and respond as Catholics?

First and foremost, we are called to be compassionate and loving to all people, regardless of any internal or personal struggles they may have. It's true that some people struggle with their gender, just as people struggle with their bodies in many other ways. These people deserve our help and support, not hatred or judgment.

With a foundation built on this charity, we are called to accept the truth and reality validated by science and God's creation. God made people male or female. All people have either XX chromosomes, and so are female, or XY, which makes them male. There's no third gender, nor can someone's gender change.

Gender confusion (including gender dysphoria and gender identity disorder) is rare at this young age before sexual awakening has occurred. Up until just a few years ago, it has been viewed as a psychological disorder. But the media have been popularizing the idea that your "feelings" about your gender should be acted upon, even if your body is the opposite sex.

Young people can become confused by what they see in the culture. When this confusion is combined with their unexplained feelings, body chemistry, and social surroundings, additional confusion and self-doubt can occur. A child with gender confusion deserves professional help, rather than to be left confused or resigned to change themselves and lead a life God did not design for them. The effects of sin, environmental factors, and emotional instability can lead a gender-confused child to be misunderstood and even mistreated by being allowed to deny his or her DNA as male or female, and eventually become "transgender" or "transsexual."

There is a normal continuum within healthy masculinity and femininity. If a young girl is a "tomboy" that doesn't mean she was meant to be a boy. It just means she is unique as a girl, and has some traits that are less common in women, though just as special and loved by God. She can still become a wonderful woman, wife, mother, or servant of God in the single life.

Likewise, if a boy is compassionate or artistic, that isn't a sign that he was meant to be a girl. He is still a boy down to his chromosomes. His interests or feelings do not mean that God created him the wrong gender. We want to encourage each child to become the best they can be, given the gender that God created them.

A child or teen's feelings about whether or not they "feel" like the gender they were born as can be the result of simple and temporary confusion or a sign of a deeper psychological problem. Many people who have attempted to surgically or hormonally alter their gender have later said that their attempt was a big mistake in the long run. While they may feel some relief or excitement at the beginning, studies show that they experience a higher rate of alcoholism, drug use, suicide, and mental illness.[17] A new study shows that the suicide rate among transgendered people who had reassignment surgery is twenty times higher than the suicide rate among non-transgender people.[18] Transgender surgery isn't the solution, because a drastic physical change doesn't address underlying psychosocial troubles. Opposing God's will in the way He created us as male and female will not bring the happiness a person desires.

The transgendered person's disorder is in the person's "assumption" or feeling that they are different than the physical reality of their body–their maleness or femaleness–as assigned by nature, and should be addressed by a professional.

To help illustrate the unchangeable basic truths on gender, here are three similar situations that can make this issue clearer.

1. An anorexic teen wants weight reduction treatment

If a dangerously thin girl suffering from anorexia looks in the mirror and thinks she is "overweight," would we say that she should have the right to gastric bypass surgery or weight reduction treatment because her feelings and self-perception tell her that she is still too fat? Should her false perceptions be accepted by society?

2. A child wants to be a puppy

A young child becomes fascinated with dogs and insists he is a puppy, barking and crawling on the ground. We know two things in this case:

- He is a child and not a dog.
- There is some emotional or psychological factor leading him to enjoy acting like a dog at this stage.

In this case, pretending can be a normal part of development. Most parents know it's likely a phase and gently remind their child of their dignity as a human, while acknowledging that it can be fun to make believe.

If the confusion were to persist, the child would need psychological help to accept the reality of his humanity. Parents recognize that their child is not, nor ever could be, a canine, despite his current desire and feeling.

3. An able-bodied person wants their healthy limbs amputated

Examples of this are rare but do occur. In cases where a person mistakenly thinks that their legs are not a real part of them and they "identify" as a paraplegic, to support their "right" to amputate them would be against the dignity and health of the human person. Currently, doctors (rightly) will not amputate healthy limbs as they have taken the Hippocratic oath to "do no harm."

In all these cases, we are called to recognize the truth of what *is*, respect the body God has given us, and do "no harm" through surgery on healthy body parts or other physical means intended to make the body appear as the opposite gender.

Some doctors who performed gender reassignment surgery on patients with the desire to help them now say that was a mistake. Dr. Paul R. McHugh, the former psychiatrist-in-chief for Johns Hopkins Hospital and current Professor of Psychiatry, based on his extensive experience in this field, now says that transgenderism is a "mental disorder" which calls for treatment, that sex change is "biologically impossible," and that people who promote sexual reassignment surgery, regardless of their intentions, are promoting a mental disorder. It is similar to a "dangerously thin" person suffering anorexia who looks in the mirror and thinks they are "overweight," said Dr. McHugh.[19]

Greater stability and happiness can be found in accepting the gender that God assigned us at conception. With proper compassion and medical and psychological help, a child can be guided to accept and thrive within his or her created gender.

It's encouraging to know that gender confused children and teens often get over their confusion on their own. Studies from Vanderbilt University and London's Portman Clinic show that

70-80 percent of children who had expressed transgender feelings "spontaneously lost those feelings" over time.[20] But for those who continue to be confused, help can be offered through psychological and/or behavioral therapy, hormones, and medicine. Parents should look for mental health professionals who align with the truth about the dignity of the human person.

For additional help, visit www.NARTH.com (National Association for the Research and Therapy of Homosexuality) or www.catholictherapists.com.

Catholic Statements on Gender Identity

"The acceptance of our bodies as God's gifts is vital for welcoming and accepting the entire world as a gift from the Father and our common home, whereas thinking that we enjoy absolute power over our own bodies turns, often subtly, into thinking that we enjoy absolute power over creation."

–Pope Francis, *Laudato Si*, 155

"The young need to be helped to accept their own body as it was created."

–Pope Francis, *Amoris Laetitia*, 285

"Biological sex and the socio-cultural role of sex (gender) can be distinguished but not separated."

–Pope Francis, *Amoris Laetitia*, 56

"Except when performed for strictly therapeutic medical reasons, directly intended amputations, mutilations, and sterilizations performed on innocent persons are against the moral law."

–*Catechism of the Catholic Church*, 2297

"The 'defense of the family' is one of the 3 biggest challenges the Church faces. The profound falsehood of this [gender] theory is so obvious. People dispute the idea that they have a nature given by their bodily identity. That serves as the defining element of the human being. They deny their nature and decide that it is not something previously given to them, but that they can make it for themselves. This denial destroys the cohesion of the family unit, specifically the role of father, mother and offspring."

–Pope Benedict XVI, Address to the Roman Curia on December 21, 2012

"According to the biblical creation account, being created by God as male and female pertains to the essence of the human creature. This duality is an essential aspect of what being human is all about, as ordained by God. This very duality as something previously given is what is now disputed. The words of the creation account: 'male and female he created them' (Gen 1:27) no longer apply [in society]. No, what applies now is this: it was not God who created them male and female—hitherto society did this, now we decide for ourselves."

–Pope Benedict XVI, Address to the Roman Curia on December 21, 2012

"Not only has God given the earth to man, who must use it with respect for the original good purpose for which it was given, but, man too is God's gift to man. He must, therefore, respect the natural and moral structure with which he has been endowed."

–Pope Francis quoting St. John Paul II, *Laudato Si*, 115

"It is not a healthy attitude which would seek to cancel out sexual difference because it no longer knows how to confront it."

–Pope Francis, *Laudato Si*, 155

"When . . . sexual differences are eliminated, we lose the anthropological basis of the family. Thus, the Holy Father speaks strongly against any gender ideology that makes one's identity as male or female merely a personal choice that can be changed over time."

–Pope Francis, *Amoris Laetitia*, 56

"'Man does not create himself.' Here is the heart of the matter. We are not the Creator."

–Pope Benedict XVI, Address to the German Parliament, Sept. 22, 2011

"The denial of the beauty of the creation of human sexuality is, in fact, a denial of the Creator of all beauty. In the end, when God's design is ignored or denied, we sow the wind of our own ideas and reap the whirlwind of confusion. Crossing the new frontier of gender identity, we court chaos."

–Bishop Serratelli, Bishop of Paterson, NJ, *Gender Identity: The New Frontier*,
Catholic News Agency, May 26, 2016

Real-Life Opportunities for Discussion

The principles we present in the *LoveEd* program can become a basis for those teachable moments that come up in the news and in daily life. Some examples follow.

Case 1: Aunt Cindy moves in with her boyfriend. Your thirteen-year-old daughter, Melanie, admires Aunt Cindy. How do you explain the situation when you want your daughter to know it's wrong, but you don't want to criticize Aunt Cindy?

Sit down and converse with Melanie. Remind her of God's plan for marriage: couples should only live together after they are married, and individuals should never use the marriage act outside of marriage. Mention that Aunt Cindy is mistaken or perhaps confused about the definitions of real love and sexual sin. Admit that many people today are also confused and mistaken about this. Then, instead of condemning Aunt Cindy, talk to Melanie about her own decisions for her future. Is she ready and willing to follow God's plan for purity? Can she act on her morals rather than her feelings? Does she have the courage to stand up against the pressure to sin? What can she do now to strengthen her determination to follow God's plan of waiting until marriage?

Case 2: Your twelve-year-old son hears the news on the car radio about the local parade for gay marriages. You are with him, and you aren't sure what to say. You want to be respectful, yet you want him to know the truth. What do you do next?

Ask him if he knows what gay marriage means to find out what he already knows. If necessary, you can explain that a homosexual attraction is toward the same sex, which is contrary to the way God created man and woman. Only a man and woman can be married since their bodies are complementary and made for each other. The only way two people can be married and have children is if they are the opposite sex; one cell comes from the man and one cell comes from the woman. Each child that exists has two biological parents: one mother and one father.

Explain to your son that the "marriage" intended by the gay agenda cannot be considered a marriage according to God's design. God already invented marriage by the way He designed a man and a woman to come together to create new life. Although God and His Church love and have compassion for people with same-sex attraction, marriage is not possible for them. Two bodies of the same sex cannot have a one-flesh union with their reproductive organs. The civil law does not have authority over God's law to make up a new definition of marriage. Then challenge your son, "If you were a senator or congressman, what would you do to help people see the common sense of God's plan?" Discuss with him how something that is legal is not always moral, but Christians are called to continue to bring true love and justice into the world.

Case 3: Your children are watching TV and a commercial comes on that is trying to sell a nonsexual product (such as toothpaste or a car) in a sexual way.

It's worth turning off the TV for a moment to have a conversation about how advertisers who try to manipulate us by stirring up sexual feelings and emotions and causing us to think we will be happy if we buy their product. If you accept it, say nothing, and let this opportunity pass, you are silently saying such advertising is okay. (Remember the prayer at Mass that says, "And what I failed to do"?) Discuss the definition of real happiness, and explain how we only find it by following God's plan for our unique lives. Brainstorm another way to advertise that product without using sex as a lure.

Case 4: You are shopping with your daughter for a new outfit. She has just grown out of girls' sizes, and you can't find anything modest.

Everything she tries on could make boys see her as a sex object; the shirts are either too tight or so low-cut so your daughter's breasts are visible from certain angles, and the skirts are so short the tops of her thighs show if she bends over. Your daughter says, "Mom, this is all they have, and everyone dresses like this anyway. It's not that bad."

Well, Mom, this is really a test of your perseverance. You could even solicit your husband's help if he wants to explain to her how men view women's bodies. Take the time to go to a different store or shop online, and be prepared to return things that don't fit properly. Show her how to layer tank tops under shirts to cover her chest area, stomach, and skirts, pants, or leggings or shorts to cover her rear end; teach her how to wear scarves or shrugs to cover the tops of low cut shirts and how to wear cute leggings under shorts and skirts. Be strong, Mom—your daughter's purity is at stake.

Case 5: A teenager writes to Coleen wanting to know if masturbation is a sin.

Hi Coleen,

I am a Catholic teenager who is wondering if the act of masturbation is still considered a sin. I have heard mixed reviews. Some say it is a sin, but I have also heard that it is a natural and healthy thing to do. Has the Church's view changed on this? I know that a vast majority of both boys and girls do it. I can understand how it would be a sin if one does it while thinking about other people, but if one is doing it to get rid of old stuff, then does it count as a sin? I have done it recently, and I am going through puberty. Is it normal to feel guilty after doing it? I love and believe in God and want to know what the views are on this issue.

Thank you,

JB

Dear JB,

Your question about masturbation is a common one, and it confuses many people. Yes, masturbation is still considered to be a sin. A small child who doesn't know it is wrong is not guilty, but his or her parents should help the child learn it is wrong. Why? Our sexual feelings are designed by God to bond us to our husband or wife in marriage. To stimulate these feelings outside of marriage teaches our mind and body that these feelings are for our own selfish pleasure. This not only offends God—who created you that way—but also can harm your sexual life in marriage later on. Acting on these sexual temptations leads to lust rather than love. Lust is using our sexual powers for the wrong purpose—selfishness. Masturbation might seem natural, and it might also be common, but it is not healthy for your body, mind, or soul.

The Church's view will not change on masturbation since this teaching is rooted in the way that our bodies are made. We were made to be a selfless gift of love to another person in marriage, not to cheapen our sexuality for selfish purposes. So, yes, it's normal to feel guilty after masturbating, because it is wrong. The priest in the confessional can offer you God's loving mercy and forgiveness as they do for any sin. Your confessor may be able to help guide you to reduce and then eliminate it if it is already a bad habit. The sacramental graces can help heal and strengthen you, so do not be afraid to confess the sin of masturbation. Almost every priest has experience in guiding people to overcome that sin.

At puberty, the sin of masturbation is often rooted in immaturity. The preteen or teen may find the sexual sensations new and pleasurable, but not be aware that God wants them to experience that pleasure with one's husband or wife in marriage only. A teen such as yourself should practice every form of self-discipline you can to overcome this sin so it does not become a habit that harms your future marriage.

Abstinence will help you mature in self-discipline as well. Why? During sexual excitement, a bonding hormone is released in your brain, and therefore habits of masturbation are a practice in bonding to your selfish pleasure rather than bonding to the person to whom you are giving your whole life. It messes with your head and with your future before you even know who your future wife might be. It sometimes can make you want to crave more and more, which can lead to sexual addition.

Mutual stimulation (touching another person sexually) is also wrong outside of marriage. All sexual touching is designed by God for a married couple as they prepare each other for the marriage act.

Masturbation is never necessary. A young man's body can naturally release excess semen through a wet dream. It is wrong for men to stimulate themselves to create an erection or to prolong an erection or to stimulate ejaculation. It is also wrong for a girl to stimulate herself for sexual sensations. All our human needs can be met in a loving way, not a sinful way.

Since you did not know this was wrong, it is not as serious of a sin, but now you know to avoid it. I'm sorry you were misinformed, but know you are not alone.

When you are tempted to masturbate, fill your life with other wholesome ideas, adventures, and activities and avoid this sin in the future. Regular exercise helps, as does turning off the TV or not listening to sexually suggestive music. Think about God, pray more, and use your body to do good deeds for others while you are going through puberty. You will be much happier practicing that kind of selfless love.

Coleen

Strong, Smart, and Pure: For Young Adolescence ⟶ Rewind

Strong: You are growing stronger as a parent. Young adolescence is an exciting time for your children as they to see how they can contribute to family, friends, and the world. They are becoming stronger in handling the changes that have occurred during puberty. They are developing their own virtues and outlooks on life, which really is part of the process of determining how they will live. You need to remain strong throughout their adolescence and not let your teens wear you down. Other good parents can feed your strength. Continue giving that good example, guide your children daily, and stay strong in your prayer life.

Smart: What you have previously taught your teens is reinforced and expanded upon with the adult topics of marriage, sexual intercourse, conception, and fetal development. Science helps them understand their sexuality and discern God's truths from the contrasting lies of the culture.

Pure: Purity is truly the gift that keeps on giving. It is given to God (as a thank-you for the life He has given them); it is given to themselves (by keeping a right and healthy perspective about relationships); and it is given as a gift to either their future spouse (by being able to give themselves to the one they marry) or to God again (in consecrated or religious life, giving a pure love to the world).

Strong, Smart, and Pure: Fast Forward ➡ Through Adolescence

Strong: You have the strength to do this!*

Smart: You have the knowledge do this!*

Pure: You have the grace to do this!*

Okay, you can only do this by the grace and strength of God . . .but LoveEd and the Church are here to help you!

Have Confidence to Educate Your Children in Love!

"A clean heart is a free heart. A free heart can love Christ with an undivided love in chastity, convinced that nothing and nobody will separate it from his love. Purity, chastity, and virginity created a special beauty in Mary that attracted God's attention. He showed his great love for the world by giving Jesus to her."

—St. Teresa of Calcutta

The following resources are included in this appendix to assist you:

- Essential Freedom to Love: The Ten Commandments
- A Nightly Spiritual Checkup for Families
- How to Pray and Some Catholic Prayers
- Quotes from the Saints About Purity
- Know the Real Definitions
- Additional Resources

It's your love that brought your child into the world. It's your love that sustains your child. It's your love that teaches him or her about God's love. It's your duty to teach your child the true meaning of love and purity. The Church is here to help you. The Vatican document *The Truth and Meaning of Human Sexuality* includes the following words of encouragement for parents:

> The Pontifical Council for the Family therefore urges parents to have confidence in their rights and duties regarding the education of their children, so as to go forward with wisdom and knowledge, knowing that they are sustained by God's gift.

In this noble task, may parents always place their trust in God through prayer to the Holy Spirit, the gentle Paraclete and Giver of all good gifts.

May they seek the powerful intercession and protection of Mary Immaculate, the Virgin Mother of fair love and model of faithful purity.

Let them also invoke Saint Joseph, her just and chaste spouse, following his example of fidelity and purity of heart.

May parents constantly rely on the love which they offer to their own children, a love which "casts out fear," which "bears all things, believes all things, hopes all things, endures all things" (1 Cor 13:7).

Such love is and must be aimed towards eternity, towards the unending happiness promised by Our Lord Jesus Christ to those who follow him: "Blessed are the pure of heart, for they shall see God" (Mt 5:8).

LoveEd covers the basics for parents to teach their child and young adolescent, but it does not cover everything your child needs to know about human sexuality before adulthood. It is part of a series of conversations with your child that can help them up until high school, when many additional resources are available for parents and schools.

As your children venture toward adulthood, your mission doesn't end.

Continue to have open, confident dialogue with them, and help your children develop responsibility. Guide them on how to intensify their faith through the struggles of daily life. Help them define in advance the virtues and conditions needed for honorable Christian union in the future.

Grow in Confidence: Knowing and Loving God's Law

The Ten Commandments Give Us the Freedom to Love.

When God first gave the Ten Commandments to Moses and God's chosen people, they were delighted. They thanked Him. Many verses in the Old Testament proclaim this appreciation with sayings such as, "How I love your law, LORD" (Ps 119:97), or, "Rather, the law of the LORD is his joy; / and on his law he meditates day and night" (Ps 1:2). Yet many people today reject the Commandments, or maybe misunderstand the gift they are to us. When we really ponder the Commandments, we see how they challenge us to be good, orderly, kind, and respectful.

The Ten Commandments are a summary of "the conditions of a life freed from the slavery of sin" (CCC 2057). Think of how many people today have become slaves to sin because they choose to disobey the commandments. It would be helpful to understand the commandments in relation to the "law of love." We know that the love of God and love of neighbor summarize all of Catholic morality. The law of love is also the first principle and source of the moral law.

The Ten Commandments are also a description of the *minimum* that love requires. Christianity itself requires much more than simply following the Ten Commandments. All Christians are further called to live the beatitudes, the virtues, and all of Christ's commands in the Gospels. If you read part 3 of the *Catechism* on the "Life in Christ," you can study more about Catholic morality in light of living God's love. What if we as a family meditated on God's law day and night as the psalmist suggests? We would probably love God even more, and learn to love our neighbor even more.

"What's 'Catholic' about the Commandments?"

While the entire Judeo-Christian tradition uses the same scriptural content for the Ten Commandments, the Protestant and Catholic list of commandments are divided differently.

Here are the Catholic Ten Commandments:

1. I am the LORD your God. You shall not have strange gods before me.

2. You shall not take the name of the LORD your God in vain.

3. Remember to keep holy the LORD's day.

4. Honor your father and your mother.

5. You shall not kill.

6. You shall not commit adultery.

7. You shall not steal.

8. You shall not bear false witness against your neighbor.

9. You shall not covet your neighbor's wife.

10. You shall not covet your neighbor's goods.

"What do those have to do with love?"

By following the Ten Commandments, we learn to train ourselves in personal freedom and self-control so that we don't do whatever we feel like doing whenever we feel like it. We are no longer slaves to our whim, but respectful to our Creator and other people who are made in His image. They are a description of the basic freedom from sin that is necessary to live and love as a Christian. They are a minimum level of living, which we should all strive to meet and then go further. The Ten Commandments provide us the freedom to live with dignity.

The Ten Commandments and Catholicism have been bound together since the time of Christ. In fact, Jesus refers to the Ten Commandments and assures their validity in His dialog with the rich young man in Matthew's Gospel (see Mt 19:16–21).

It's important to note that each commandment is simply a *summary* of a whole category of actions. Instead of being legalistic, searching for a way around them if their wording doesn't fit us perfectly, we should look at them as steps to mastering ourselves so that our life can truly be a gift back to God and to others. For example, "bearing false witness against your neighbor" covers any kind of falsehood: perjury, lying, slander, rash judgment, etc. It also covers gossip, detraction, or anything that can harm a person's reputation. Avoiding these sins leads us toward a life of virtue.

The commandments express man's fundamental duties to love God and neighbor. As such, they represent *serious* obligations. To violate them knowingly and willingly in a significant way is to commit mortal sin (see CCC 1858-59) If you want to learn how to follow them better, and teach your children well, the *Catechism of the Catholic Church* has a detailed description of each of the Ten Commandments (CCC 2052). Take time to read it as a family and delight in God's law of love!

Grow in Confidence: Help Your Children Form Their Consciences

Your Nightly Family Checkup: An Examination of Conscience

Your nightly family checkup, usually called an examination of conscience, could begin with some simple questions about following the commandments, and then it could deepen as you study the *Catechism* more and develop a deeper spirituality as individuals, as a couple, and as a family. Your children will benefit by properly forming their consciences early in their lives.

A sample nightly checkup could include the commandments in a simple question format.

First, ask the Holy Spirit to help you see yourself as God sees you, imperfect yet lovable. Seek His mercy each day as you examine your consciences together:

1. Did we put God first today? Did we say our prayers, ask Him for help, and think of Him while we worked and played?

2. Did we speak well of God and only use His name reverently? Did the language we used today glorify God?

3. Did we go to Mass on Sunday? Did we plan our Sunday around godly activities such as nature walks, spiritual readings, or wholesome family entertainment that drew us closer together in love?

4. Were we good parents today? Were our children obedient today? Did we teach our children to obey us and all authority? Did we honor our own parents and offer them the care they need for their age?

5. Maybe we didn't kill anybody today, but were we kind and patient? Did we spiritually "kill" another with constant criticism or badgering? Did we get drunk or take harmful drugs?

6. Did we carefully screen our entertainment today to avoid influences that are impure or that make sexual sin appear to be casual and normal? Were we faithful and kind to our spouse today in our thoughts, words, and deeds?

7. Did we give an honest day's work today, not stealing time from our employer? Did we return everything we had borrowed? Did we ask permission before taking something out of another family member's room?

8. Did we tell any lies we have to confess? Were we prudent and honest with one another? Did we avoid gossip or speaking badly about someone?

9. Did we avoid impure thoughts, filling our minds with goodness, truth, and beauty?

10. Did we promote fairness and justice in our family today, only buying what we need, avoiding excess and greed? Were we careful not to waste our hard-earned money and keep within a budget?

Also, the two great commandments (see Lk 10:27):

1. Did I love God today with all my heart, all my soul, all my strength, and all my mind?

2. Did I love my neighbor as myself?

Then pray an Act of Contrition together. This is a good prayer before bedtime when you are sorry for your sins and at each sacramental confession.

Oh my God, I am heartily sorry for having offended you.

I detest all my sins because I dread the loss of heaven and the pains of hell.

But most of all, because they offend you, my God

Who are all good and deserving of all my love.

I firmly resolve, with the help of your grace,

To confess my sins, to do penance, and to amend my life. Amen.

Grow in Confidence by Praying to God

Never underestimate the power of God. He loves you, and He can do anything! The closer you get to Him in prayer, the more you will see His presence in your life. Then, you will want to pray even more, out of love rather than duty. God loves you! Prayer connects us to God. It opens our hearts and minds to God Himself, to His word, and to His will for us. If we want to be confident in teaching our children and living out our faith as a family, we need to stay connected to God.

How do we pray? Jesus's apostles asked Him that very question. In the Sermon on the Mount, Jesus taught us to pray to "Our Father, who art in heaven."

Overcoming Common Myths About Prayer

Have you ever heard anyone say . . .

"I just can't find the time to pray."

"I don't need to pray in any 'formal' sense. God knows I love Him."

"I don't get anything out of it."

"I've tried learning how to pray, but I just don't get it. It's too hard."

People have many excuses to skip prayer when they don't make it a priority. Even if you have a houseful of active kids, or too much homework, or a job that consumes way too much of your time, you can still pray.

The truth is that prayer is Good News! Who else loves you unconditionally? Who else is longing to hear your voice? Who else is just waiting to hear from you any day or time?

With God, you don't need an appointment, a phone, a computer, or a charged battery. Just bring Him your heart, open it up, and let Him love you, and tell Him you love Him in return. A prayer life is *essential* to the Christian life; it is "a vital and personal relationship with the living and true God" (CCC 2558). Prayer is the lifeblood of your faith. Without prayer, your faith will die (see CCC 2744).

Prayer Is Compatible With Everyday Life

We all need to set aside a small amount of quiet time each day to pray. But it's not difficult—just five or ten minutes to start is fine. Make prayer a part of the fabric of your everyday life. You can lift up your mind and talk to God anytime: when you're waiting in the car, taking a break from work, or even *while* working, you can find God in all the normal tasks of daily life. Seek Him there.

St. John Chrysostom once said, "It is possible to offer fervent prayer even while walking in public or strolling alone, or seated in your shop, . . . while buying or selling, . . . or even while cooking."

Even the Smallest Faith Will Blossom Through Prayer

Your faith will grow when you make prayer a daily habit, guaranteed! You show up and God will do the work. He wants to be with you and listen to you and respond to you. Then when you hear Him and see His responses in life's circumstances, you'll say, "Now I see God in that circumstance."

If you think you don't have enough faith to pray, know that God is here to help. It is the devil who doesn't want you to pray and the Holy Spirit who helps you pray. St. Paul tells us, "The Spirit, too, comes to the aid of our weakness; for we do not know how to pray as we ought, but the Spirit itself intercedes with inexpressible groanings" (Rom 8:26). Even sighing to God is a prayer!

God sometimes works on a slower timetable, just like nature. You can't rush a plant to grow, but when it does, you are amazed at the flowers and fruits that came out of the small seed. So start praying now for your child's purity and their capacity to love, even though they haven't started dating yet. Pray for your child daily and on every step of the way in this journey toward love, and pray for yourself for the strength to lead them. Be faithful, and you will see results in God's time.

Learning How to Pray Is Simple

The basics of prayer are simple. Throughout the ages, people have learned to pray in all kinds of circumstances. Sometimes we feel good in prayer, and sometimes we don't feel anything at all. Remember that even saints had dry times of prayer. Make the effort to pray anyway, and if distractions come, say the name of Jesus and focus on Him.

Verbal Prayer may be memorized prayers from childhood, the Rosary, a novena of nine prayers for a certain intention, or a spontaneous talking to God from your heart. Tell Him your concerns, and even though He already knows them, offer your problems to Him and let Him carry them to lighten your load.

Meditation Prayer is a Godly reflection on the Scriptures, *Catechism*, and writings of the saints. Just read and ponder His truths in all the ways they come to you. You can even meditate on the attributes of God our Creator in the beauty of nature.

Contemplative prayer is a gift from God that we read about in the lives of the saints. But it's not just reserved for saints. It's that deep heart-to-heart connection with God. Anyone can receive the gift of contemplative union with God when we visit Him frequently and stay close to Him in love. Contemplative prayer is a simple surrender of your heart to God's will, knowing that He loves you deeply. It's a silent and personal attentiveness to God, uniting you to Him.

Catholic Prayers for Purity

Prayer to the Holy Spirit

(Good to use before reading the Scriptures or before examining your conscience)

Come Holy Spirit, fill the hearts of your faithful and kindle in them the fire of your love. Send forth your Spirit and they shall be created. And you shall renew the face of the earth.

O, God, who by the light of the Holy Spirit, did instruct the hearts of the faithful, grant that by the same Holy Spirit, we may be truly wise and ever enjoy His consolations, through Christ Our Lord. Amen.

St. Augustine's Prayer to the Holy Spirit

Breathe in me, O Holy Spirit, that my thoughts may all be holy. Act in me, O Holy Spirit, that my work, too, may be holy. Draw my heart, O Holy Spirit, that I love but what is holy. Strengthen me, O Holy Spirit, to defend all that is holy. Guard me, then, O Holy Spirit, that I always may be holy. Amen.

Prayer to St. Michael the Archangel

Saint Michael, the Archangel, defend us in battle. Be our protection against the wickedness and snares of the devil. May God rebuke him, we humbly pray; and do you, O Prince of the heavenly host, by the power of God cast into hell Satan and all the evil spirits who wander through the world seeking the ruin of souls. Amen.

Prayer for Purity

Jesus, Lover of chastity, Mary, Mother most pure, and Joseph, chaste guardian of the Virgin, to you I come at this hour, begging you to plead with God for me. I earnestly wish to be pure in thought, word and deed in imitation of your own holy purity.

Obtain for me, then, a deep sense of modesty which will be reflected in my external conduct. Protect my eyes, the windows of my soul, from anything that might dim the luster of a heart that must mirror only Christ-like purity.

And when the "Bread of Angels becomes the Bread of me" in my heart at Holy Communion, seal it forever against the suggestions of sinful pleasures.

Heart of Jesus, Fount of all purity, have mercy on us.

Grow in Confidence: God's Plan Is the Best!

Each year . . .

Millions of teens do not catch sexually transmitted diseases.

Millions do not suffer heartache or depression from broken sexual relationships.

Millions of teens do not get pregnant outside of marriage.

Millions look away from pornography.

Millions of teens use respectful language.

. . . Because they are all practicing *Chastity*!

Millions of teens can make a difference, one at a time, one relationship at a time. God's plan for love and chastity is possible, livable, and good!

Grow in Confidence: Inspiring Quotes From the Saints

The struggle to teach and live purity is not new to the Church. God's grace has been with the Church throughout the centuries to assist all who believe and wish to practice purity. Many saints have struggled and won the battle for purity. They have plenty of advice to share with our children and us. You know which quotes will inspire your child the most, so read them together and have them choose their favorite. Have your child write one on a sticky note, print on a bookmark or placemat, or make into screensavers as daily encouragement.

"We must be pure. I do not speak merely of the purity of the senses. We must observe great purity in our will, in our intentions, in all our actions."

–St. Peter Julian Eymard

"God desires from you the least degree of purity of conscience more than all the works you can perform."

–St. John of the Cross

"Holy Purity, the queen of virtues, the angelic virtue, is a jewel so precious that those who possess it become like the angels of God in heaven, even though clothed in mortal flesh."

–St. John Bosco

"Those whose hearts are pure are the temples of the Holy Spirit."

–St. Lucy

"God demands great purity of certain souls, and so He gives them a deeper knowledge of their own misery. Illuminated by light from on high, the soul can better know what pleases God and what does not."

–St. Faustina, *Divine Mercy in My Soul*, 112

"Only the chaste man and the chaste woman are capable of true love."

—St. John Paul II

"In the realm of evil thoughts none induces to sin as much as do thoughts that concern the pleasure of the flesh."

—St. Thomas Aquinas

"In temptations against chastity, the spiritual masters advise us, not so much to contend with the bad thought, as to turn the mind to some spiritual, or, at least, indifferent object. It is useful to combat other bad thoughts face to face, but not thoughts of impurity."

—St. Alphonsus Liguori

"[God] has assigned as a duty to every man the dignity of every woman."

—St. John Paul II

"To be pure, to remain pure, can only come at a price, the price of knowing God and loving him enough to do his will. He will always give us the strength we need to keep purity as something as beautiful for him."

—St. Teresa of Calcutta

"Blessed the one who loves holiness like the light and has not defiled his body with dark deeds of the Evil One in the sight of the Lord."

—St. Ephrem of Syria

"Lust indulged became habit, and habit unresisted, became necessity."

—St. Augustine

"There is need for a crusade of manliness and purity to counteract and nullify the savage work of those who think man is a beast. And that crusade is your work."

—St. Josemaría Escrivá

"We must practice modesty, not only in our looks, but also in our whole deportment, and particularly in our dress, our walk, our conversation, and all similar actions."

—St. Alphonsus Maria de Liguori

"When you decide firmly to lead a clean life, chastity will not be a burden on you: it will be a crown of triumph."

—St. Josemaría Escrivá

"When you have sought the company of a sensual satisfaction, what loneliness afterward!"

—St. Josemaría Escrivá

"Don't say, 'That's the way I am—it's my character.' It's your lack of character. *Esto vir!*—Be a man!"

—St. Josemaría Escrivá

"Purity is the fruit of prayer."

–St. Teresa of Calcutta

"Purity prepares the soul for love, and love confirms the soul in purity."

–Blessed John Henry Cardinal Newman

"More souls go to hell because of sins of the flesh than for any other reason."

–Our Lady of Fatima

"Filthy talk makes us feel comfortable with filthy action. But the one who knows how to control the tongue is prepared to resist the attacks of lust."

–St. Clement of Alexandria

"Never talk of impure things or events, not even to deplore them. Look, it's a subject that sticks more than tar. Change the conversation, or if that's not possible, continue, but speaking of the need and beauty of holy purity–a virtue of the men who know what their souls are worth."

–St. Josemaría Escrivá

"The man of impure speech is a 'person whose lips are but an opening and a supply pipe which hell uses to vomit its impurities upon the earth.'"

–St. John Marie Vianney

"Either we must speak as we dress, or dress as we speak. Why do we profess one thing and display another? The tongue talks of chastity, but the whole body reveals impurity."

–St. Jerome

"Far be it from Christians that to do such deeds [as are done by pagan sinners] should enter their mind; for temperance dwells with them, self-restraint is practiced, monogamy is observed, chastity is guarded, injustice is exterminated, sin is rooted out, righteousness is exercised, law is ministered, reverence is preserved, God is acknowledged: truth controls, grace guards, peace protects, the holy word guides, wisdom teaches, life directs, God reigns."

–Saint Theophilus of Antioch

"He alone loves the Creator perfectly who manifests a pure love for his neighbor."

–St. Bede the Venerable

"The pure soul is a beautiful rose, and the Three Divine Persons descend from Heaven to inhale its fragrance."

–St. John Marie Vianney

"Now the purity of man is chastity, which is called honesty, and the observance of it, honor and also integrity; and its contrary is called corruption; in short, it has this peculiar excellence above the other virtues, that it preserves both soul and body fair and unspotted."

–St. Francis de Sales

"Chastity, or cleanness of heart, holds a glorious and distinguished place among the virtues, because she, alone, enables man to see God; hence Truth itself said, 'Blessed are the clean of heart, for they shall see God.'"

—St. Augustine

"There is no remedy so powerful against the heat of concupiscence as the remembrance of our Savior's Passion. In all my difficulties I never found anything so efficacious as the wounds of Christ: In them I sleep secure; from them I derive new life."

—St. Augustine

"Humility is the safeguard of chastity. In the matter of purity, there is no greater danger than not fearing the danger. For my part, when I find a man secure of himself and without fear, I give him up for lost. I am less alarmed for one who is tempted and who resists by avoiding the occasions [of sin], than for one who is not tempted and is not careful to avoid occasions. When a person puts himself in an occasion saying, I shall not fall, it is an almost infallible sign that he will fall, and with great injury to his soul."

—St. Philip Neri

"The state of grace is nothing other than purity, and it gives heaven to those who clothe themselves in it. Holiness, therefore, is simply the state of grace purified, illuminated, beautified by the most perfect purity, exempt not only from mortal sin but also from the smallest faults; purity will make saints of you! Everything lies in this!"

—St. Peter Eymard

Grow in Confidence: Key Definitions

Adultery: Sexual relations between a married person and someone to whom he or she is not married; sometimes used as a general term to include all sexual relations outside of marriage (see fornication).

Celibacy: Abstention from sexual relations. In the case of the priesthood or religious life, celibacy is a sign of a greater union, a spousal relationship, directly with God and His bride, the Church.

Cervix: The lower part (neck) of the uterus.

Chastity: A virtue that helps protect love from selfishness and aggressiveness; the virtue of refraining from sexual intimacies before marriage; being faithful to your spouse through your whole life and open to life during marriage; part of the cardinal virtue of temperance.

Co-create: The act of creating new human life *with God*.

Conception: The moment when the sperm cell joins the egg cell and human life begins.

Conjugal Union: The personal and physical union enjoyed by a man and wife, including the sexual embrace that is both procreative and unitive. Conjugal love is the joining love of two persons, not just two bodies.

Custody of the Eyes: Managing what one sees, particularly looking away from immodest or indecent pictures or videos.

Ejaculation: The release of sperm and semen through the penis to the outside of the body.

Embryo: The term used for the baby while growing in its mother's womb for the first three months. In the last six months, it is called a fetus.

Erection: Increased firmness and size of the penis due to the blood vessels filling up inside, usually due to stress or excitement.

Fallopian Tubes: Tubal passages extending from the uterus to the ovaries that help transport the egg cell (ovum) to the uterus during ovulation each month; the site of conception.

Fertility: The power to transmit human life in a biological way. Men are usually fertile from puberty until death, since sperm production is ongoing. Women are normally fertile from puberty to around age fifty (menopause)–about one week per month, surrounding the days when the egg is released from the ovary.

Fertilization: The moment when a male sperm enters a female ovum as a child is conceived.

Fetus: A developing child from the third month of gestation in the womb until birth.

Fornication: Biblical term for premarital sex that includes sexual activities outside of marriage. It includes premarital sex, masturbation, oral sex, and any sexual foreplay outside of marriage.

Fortitude: Mental and emotional strength in facing difficulty, adversity, danger, or temptation; the courage to resist evil and do good.

Genitals: The organs designed by God that make up the reproductive system and can generate new life. In men: penis, testicles, and scrotum; in women: vulva, vagina, fallopian tubes, ovaries, uterus.

Holy: Dedicated or devoted to the service of God, the Church, or religion; a holy person: being saintly, godly, pious, and devout.

Hormone: A chemical compound produced by the glands and carried to the site of action by the bloodstream; hormones influence the growth and function of various parts of the body.

Immaculate Conception: The feast day of the Church that celebrates the Catholic dogma that Mary was without original sin on her soul from the moment of her conception in her mother's womb.

Justice: The quality of being fair and morally righteous; to uphold the justice of a cause; rightfulness or lawfulness, as of a claim or title; in the moral principle, giving to God what is owed to Him and to others what they are due.

Mature: The full development of a person, including one's physical, emotional, mental, social, and spiritual dimensions.

Menopause: The natural time in a woman's life, after her childbearing years (around fifty years old), when she experiences bodily changes that leave her infertile, meaning she can no longer mature and release egg cells, and she can no longer conceive a child.

Menstruation: The periodic discharge of blood and mucosal tissue from the uterus out of the body through the vagina, usually occurring monthly from puberty to menopause in non-pregnant women.

Modesty: Acting with regard for decency of behavior, speech, dress, etc.; not wearing revealing or suggestive clothing; freedom from vanity, boastfulness, showing off, etc.

Nocturnal Emission: The natural release of semen during sleep, which may be accompanied by dreams about women during the years of puberty. This natural release through the penis to the outside of the body, or any accompanying erection, is not harmful, nor is it to be intentionally prolonged.

Ovaries: The female glands that produce hormones and contain ovum in which the ova (egg cells) reach maturity.

Ovum: A mature egg cell from the female ovary.

Penis: The male organ that provides for the release of urine or semen.

Period: (see Menstruation).

Pituitary Gland: The master endocrine gland near the brain affecting all hormonal functions in the body; it secretes hormones (chemical messengers) to other parts of the body.

Placenta: The organ that nourishes the developing fetus in the womb, which develops from the baby to attach to the inside of the mother's uterus.

Pregnancy: The usual period of nine months during which a developing fetus is carried within the uterus; it begins at conception and ends at birth.

Procreation/Procreate: To beget or generate offspring; to bring new life into being with God.

Prostate Gland: A chestnut-shaped body surrounding the urethra in the male; it contributes a secretion to semen.

Prudence: The quality of being cautious with regard to practical matters, using discretion for what we say or do; thinking before we speak or act.

Puberty: A time of rapid growth and great physical change for boys and girls as they become men and women; the age at which a person is first capable of sexual reproduction of offspring.

Purity: To be solely focused on God's love, untainted by sexual sin; freedom from anything that debases, contaminates, pollutes, etc.

Reproductive System: The system of bodily organs that function in a man or a woman that can assist God in bringing new human life into the world.

Reverence: An attitude of deep respect, tinted with awe; veneration; a gesture indicating deep respect, usually shown toward God and holy or well-respected people.

Scrotum: A soft pouch of skin on the outside of the male body that contains the testes.

Self-Mastery: Having self-control over one's impulses; acting with thoughtfulness toward God's plan for one's sexuality; moral use of one's sexual powers.

Semen: The fluid that helps transport sperm (the male reproductive cells).

Sexual Intercourse: The physical union of the male and female sexual organs. Also called the Marriage Act or the Conjugal Union.

Sexuality: The maleness of a man or femaleness of a woman; masculinity or femininity and how it is lived out for the whole person, body, mind, and soul. Sexuality begins with the chromosomal structure of XX for the female and XY for the male.

Temperance: Moderation or self-restraint in action, speech, eating, or drinking; self-control; balance.

Testes: Two ball-shaped organs in a male, which produce sperm cells and hormones, and hang gently outside the body in the scrotum between the legs.

Uterus: The pear-shaped organ inside a female that can nourish and hold a developing baby during pregnancy; also called the womb.

Virginity: The state of being sexually pure; avoidance of all sexual activity.

Vocation: God's call to a certain state of life for each individual; one's path to heaven; lived out through either marriage or celibacy.

Wet Dream: (see nocturnal emission).

XX and XY Chromosomes: pairs of genetic DNA that biologically determine a person's sex at their conception as either male or female. People with XX chromosomes are females and people with XY chromosomes are males.

Additional Resources

Five more books that are part of this LoveEd series:
- LoveEd: Facilitator Guide
- Boy's Guide: Level 1
- Boy's Guide: Level 2
- Girl's Guide: Level 1
- Girl's Guide: Level 2

*Level 1 is recommended for children ages 9–11, and Level 2 for ages 11–14. All products are available through www.SaintBenedictPress.com.

Vatican and Papal Documents at www.vatican.va:
- *Truth and Meaning of Human Sexuality*, Pontifical Council for the Family
- *Familiaris Consortio*, Pope St. John Paul II (On the Role of the Christian Family in the Modern World)
- *Humanae Vitae*, Pope Paul VI (On Human Life)
- *Deus Caritas Est*, Pope Benedict XVI (God is Love)
- *Theology of the Body*, Pope St. John Paul II

United States Conference of Catholic Bishops Documents
- Marriage and Family Enrichment articles from the USCCB www.foryourmarriage.org
- *Catechetical Formation in Chaste Living,* A document from the Bishops of the US, prepared by the Committee on Evangelization and Catechesis. www.usccb.org
- Human Life and Dignity Teachings. http://www.usccb.org/issues-and-action/human-life-and-dignity
- National Pastoral Initiatives for Marriage. http://www.usccb.org/issues-and-action/marriage-and-family/national-pastoral-intitiative-for-marriage.cfm

Resource websites

www.sexrespect.com
From the author of *LoveEd*, this provides additional chastity and abstinence programs, with a detailed parent guidebooks for older teens' questions. It includes topics such as how to know if you are ready to date, romance, attraction, infatuation and love, how to resist temptation, real love quizzes, a pledge for teen purity, and more detailed biological and moral information.

www.respect4u.com
Promotes the messages of character, chastity, and family life.

www.cultureoflifestudies.com
Prolife lessons, activities, and videos from American Life League.

www.sisterkieransawyer.com
Teen sexuality and child protection programs.

www.chastity.com
The well-known Jason and Crystalina Evert's website.

www.sexualwisdom.com
Dr. Richard Wetzel's free books for older teens and adults on the medical aspects of sexual integrity.

www.JPIIHealingCenter.org
Dr. Bob Schuchts's ministry, including Healing the Whole Person retreats and resources.

www.narth.com
National Association for the Research and Therapy of Homosexuality

www.TakeBackMarriage.org
Marriage Reality Movement - Individuals and organizations working to take back marriage for our children and families. Learn how to communicate the reality of marriage without conflict or confusion so that family and friends can understand.

http://TOBET.org
Theology of the Body Evangelization Team (TOBET) shares the life-affirming Theology of the Body message through educational resources–books, programs, talks, and seminars–to offer hope and healing to a culture in need.

http://tobinstitute.org
Theology of the Body Institute offers Theology of the Body courses, a certification program, a clergy enrichment program, speakers, and much more.

http://corproject.com/
Cor Project is a global outreach founded by Christopher West, the world's most recognized teacher of John Paul II's *Theology of the Body*, with the aim of helping men and women learn, live, and share the beauty and splendor of God's plan for life, love, and sexuality.

www.ccli.org
The Couple to Couple League teaches Natural Family Planning.

www.fertilitycare.org
International practitioners that assist with NFP as well as Naprotechnology as a moral form of fertility treatments that respect the dignity of the persons.

www.catholictherapists.com
National network of psychiatrists, therapists, and life coaches who help clients approach life with Catholic values.

www.thekingsmen.org
Local parish groups around the world providing a support system for healthy fatherhood, authentic masculinity, and purity.

www.catholicgentleman.net
An online blog for men that seeks to encourage virtue, holiness, and true masculinity.

Resources for prevention and treatment of pornography use

- Internet-filtering software: Covenant Eyes, Mobicip, Net Nanny, Screen Retriever, and K9 Web Protection.
- *Good Pictures Bad Pictures: Porn-Proofing Today's Young Kids* by Kirsten Jenson and Gail Poyner www.protectyoungminds.org
- integrityrestored.com
- provenmen.org
- bravehearts.net

For additional info on teaching teens chastity, sexuality, and dating at the next level, read *Love and Life: A Christian Sexual Morality Guide for Teens*. Available from Ignatius Press.

Endnotes

1. Pope John Paul II. *The Role of the Christian Family in the Modern World* (Familiaris Consortio), November 22, 1981, p. 36.

2. Pontifical Council for the Family, *The Truth and Meaning of Human Sexuality: Guidelines for Education within the Family* (www.vatican.va) 1996, p. 145.

3. United States Conference of Catholic Bishops, *Catechetical Formation in Chaste Living*, page 22.

4. *Truth and Meaning*, n. 1, 6.

5. Vatican Congregation of the Doctrine of the Faith, *The Dignity of the Person*, 2008, n. 6.

6. Paul VI. *Encyclical Letter on the Regulation of Birth* (*Humanae Vitae*), July 25, 1968. n. 10, 16.

7. *Truth and Meaning*, n. 17.

8. *Ibid.*, n. 105.

9. *Formation in Chaste Living*, n. 26.

10. St. Pope John Paul II, Homily at Santa Clara, Cuba, 1998. www.vatican.va.

11. *Truth and Meaning*, n. 65-75.

12. *Ibid.*, n. 121-127.

13. *Ibid.*, n. 78.

14. *Ibid.*, p. 83.

15. Congregation for Catholic Education, *Educational Guidance in Human Love*, n. 58.

16. Ministry to Persons with Homosexual Inclination. 2006.

17. Jerome Hunt, "Why the Gay and Transgender Population Experiences Higher Rates of Substance Abuse," *Center for American Progress*. Published March 9, 2012. Accessed on April 18, 2017. https://www.americanprogress.org/issues/lgbt/reports/2012/03/09/11228/why-the-gay-and-transgender-population-experiences-higher-rates-of-substance-use/.

18. Tyler Carpenter, "Is America Normalizing Mental Illness?" *The Review: The Independent Student Voice of Utah Valley University*. Published February 22, 2017. Accessed on April 18, 2017. http://www.uvureview.com/recent/opinions/is-america-normalizing-mental-illness/.

19. Dr. Paul McHugh, "Transgender Surgery Isn't the Solution," *The Wall Street Journal*. Published May 13, 2016. Accessed on April 18, 2017. https://www.wsj.com/articles/paul-mchugh-transgender-surgery-isnt-the-solution-1402615120.

20. *Ibid.*